Kelly Gibney is an Auckland-based cook, food stylist, photographer and mother of two who loves to chat, slurp noodles and make friends with dogs.

Over the last decade, her recipes and photography have appeared in *Dish Magazine*, *Fashion Quarterly*, *NZ Herald* and *Stuff*. She has also collaborated with many of New Zealand's most-loved food brands.

Kelly has appeared on THREE and TVNZ and you'll regularly hear her on RNZ.

Kelly's background was previously in hospitality in New York, Melbourne and Auckland. She has been a judge for *Metro* magazine's Restaurant of the Year Awards and she enjoys hosting and MCing food and hospitality industry-related events. Her debut cookbook *Wholehearted* was released in 2017. Her recipes have also been published in *Whole* and *The RNZ Cookbook*.

ENJOY

KELLY GIBNEY

FOOD WORTH SHARING WITH THE PEOPLE YOU LOVE

Beatnik

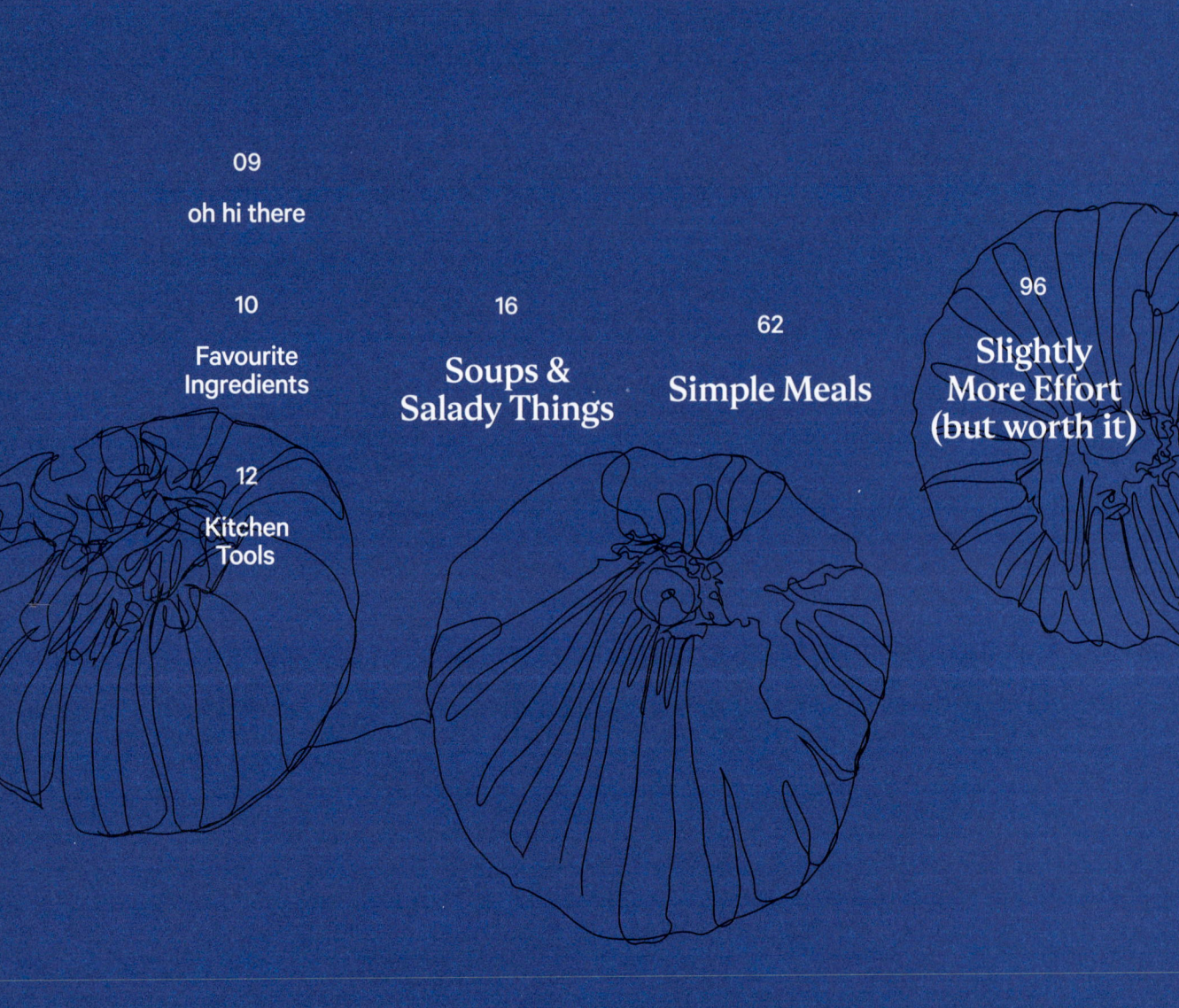

09 oh hi there

10 Favourite Ingredients

12 Kitchen Tools

16 Soups & Salady Things

62 Simple Meals

96 Slightly More Effort (but worth it)

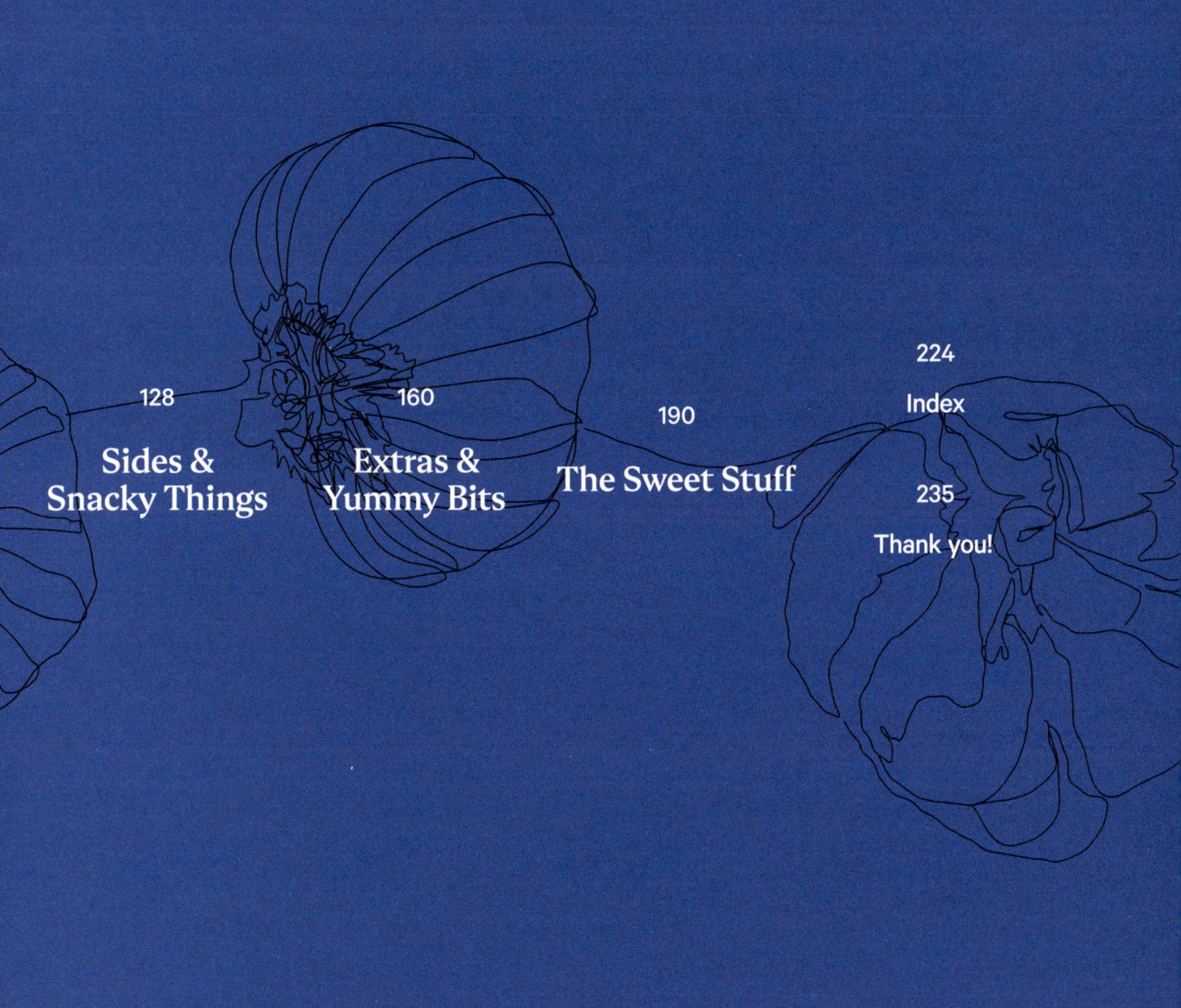

128
Sides & Snacky Things

160
Extras & Yummy Bits

190
The Sweet Stuff

224
Index

235
Thank you!

While trying my hardest not to be overly earnest (I'm guilty of this sometimes), I can't tell you how excited I am to share my cookbook with you. I've made it with so much love. Everything was dreamt up, cooked, shot, edited and written in my home. When the deadline came around I found it hard to hand it over and say goodbye to a project I've been enjoying so much. Seven years on from writing my debut cookbook *Wholehearted,* it's been so cool to see my growth and honed point of view as a cook, photographer, stylist - and as a human. (After all, I'm a mature, wise woman of 42 now!)

Although I didn't realise it at the time, the seeds of this cookbook were planted in the covid lockdowns of 2020 and 2021. We were all told to stay at home and life became very simple in some ways. With Luke not working late or any after-school activities for our daughters, for the first time ever we were able to have a family dinner every single night. Coming together around a table for a home-cooked meal at that time had made a profound impact on us as a family and me as a cook.

My kitchen endeavours felt they had a deepened purpose as I cooked to distract and delight my little family during an uncertain time. The food wasn't complicated or fancy but dinner was the anchor of our day and we all looked forward to it immensely. Over those months we tried and discovered new family favourites. I cooked my way through all my beloved childhood dishes and my daughters' tastes expanded as they got more adventurous.

Around that time I started talking to Sally and Rachel from Beatnik about doing another book but was struggling to come up with a theme or focus that felt right.

I was cooking with my older daughter one day, teaching her to make a meal she loved, and I snapped a picture of it. I saw this picture of Bonnie holding the smoky beans we'd made and it kind of hit me over the head - "this is my next book". This was the only honest option for me: family food. Simple, homemade food. The food we eat and enjoy together. While I'd been trying to come up with a clever concept, I'd overlooked the everyday food that was bringing me purpose and pleasure daily.

I've always been passionate about good nutrition but the meals in this book are about so much more. We have been creating our own traditions and we, like every family, have been chasing that elusive thing - the meal we all love. There's such joy and triumph in finding a recipe that everyone around the table, big and small, despite different tastes, can enthuse about and look forward to. I really hope this book delivers some of those mealtime wins to your household.

This of course doesn't need to be with family members. It can be with flatmates, friends, or whoever you like to share good food with.

I won't be as flippant as to suggest that a home-cooked meal will make the worries or ups and downs of life disappear but, when things are tough and a bit gloomy, returning to the basics of coming together with the people we enjoy spending time with and eating the foods we love goes a long way to soothing and even insulating us (albeit for a moment) from all that goes on in the world.

One of my favourite meals of this past summer was a simple and very delicious meal of homemade gnocchi in tomato sauce served by friends. The evening was bright and clear after a period of bad weather and awful flooding in Auckland. We sat outside on their terrace and the food was presented on plates our friend Ellie had made. The lovely meal and the good company was just the thing we all needed after an unsettling time.

Food is a magnificent medium. It carries memories, conveys love and affection, heals, soothes and excites. I feel incredibly lucky to have the creation and capturing of food as my creative outlet. I have so much fun doing what I do. It's such a gift.

I hope, as all cookbook authors do, that this book will be infinitely useful for you. That it will bring you cooking inspiration, some distraction from the world as you flip its pages and some great eating and sharing.

– Love Kelly x

MY FAVOURITE INGREDIENTS

These are the ingredients I will always have on hand. They make my everyday cooking really sing.

BUTTER

Butter is the best. It makes everything taste better. All the recipes in this book use regular salted butter unless I've stated otherwise. That's the butter I always have on hand and I find it works well for most things that I make, even baking. Butter has become quite expensive here in New Zealand in recent years so I don't see any reason to have unsalted butter in the fridge unless I'm using it regularly.

CHICKPEAS

Canned chickpeas are something I always have in my pantry. I love them for whipping up homemade hummus (so good when it's freshly made). Chickpeas are brilliant for making chilli, curries and chunky soups go a little further. They add protein and great texture.

DRIED CHILLI FLAKES

I use fresh chillies a lot but dried chilli flakes can't be beaten as a pantry staple because they keep for so long. They're essential in making my beloved Chilli & Garlic Oil (pg 170) and fabulous for livening up all sorts of dishes. I scatter a pinch over eggs and soups, I stir some through grain salads, and, of course, many pasta dishes love a generous pinch of dried chilli flakes.

DRIED HERBS

Not the poor cousin of fresh herbs, dried herbs are an absolute pantry essential because they guarantee you'll always have some good herb options on hand.

The dried version of herbs such as tarragon and dill, which I love the flavour of but don't consistently have fresh, are especially handy. The shelf life of dried herbs, though long, is not endless. Keep an eye out for diminishing colour and flavour. Those stored in airtight containers will last longer than those in poorly sealed bags or little boxes.

FREE RANGE EGGS

What would I do without the incredibly versatile and hardworking egg? It's hard to imagine leaning on another ingredient as much as we do eggs. I love them. They're relatively affordable, loved by most and can be prepared in countless ways. I often have eggs and vegetables for breakfast, or I'll make my egg salad (pg 146) for lunch. If dinner time rolls around and I find myself without a plan, eggs will often ride to the rescue.

FRESH HERBS

Having a couple of different types of fresh herbs on hand will make all the difference to your cooking. There are few savoury dishes that are not improved with their addition. Slow-cooked meaty dishes benefit hugely from freshly picked parsley added at the end and salads really sing when tossed with fresh mint and basil leaves. For me, the trinity of ingredients that most lift a dish are the addition of fresh herbs, citrus juice or zest and a good salt seasoning. Magical.

LEMONS AND LIMES

I'm never without lemons. Citrus season is my favourite time of year, even though it heralds the start of the colder months, because I love when my fruit bowl is full of lemons and limes. A squeeze of citrus juice brightens up most dishes. Soups and curries especially taste better with a hit of citrus at the end.

And citrus zest is sensational in all the places you want a little fresh sharpness, such as stews, cakes and through grains,

OLIVE OIL

Olive oil is the lifeblood of my kitchen. I always have a standard olive oil on hand for sautéing, frying and roasting. A light olive oil for homemade mayo (its less intense flavour is better for this) and then a REALLY good extra virgin olive oil for drizzling on everything and using in salad dressings.

SALT

I use fine salt in my recipes and always have flaky sea salt on hand for that finishing flourish on top. Making sure your cooking is well seasoned makes a huge difference to the finished result. In a health sense I don't shy away from using salt. Consuming a lot of salt from processed food is another thing altogether, but when it comes to home cooking, season to accentuate all that effort you've put in.

SOY SAUCE & TAMARI

These two things are not the same (tamari is brewed without wheat) but I use them often, and to be honest, interchangeably. I like having a few options on hand in this category because it's a condiment that I love. I'll usually have an organic tamari, a nice Japanese soy sauce, a dark soy for stir fry sauces and then we've got a favourite, very tasty (more processed / longer ingredient list) Chinese light soy sauce that we love with dumplings and in noodle soups. Tamari and soy sauce are a brilliant amplifier of umami (that magical savoury note) in dishes. I use it in more unlikely places like spaghetti bolognese and in curries. I'll add a little of it to the egg dip when I'm making schnitzel and crumbed tofu and I love scrambled eggs with a little soy sauce, sesame oil, chilli and spring onion added before cooking.

SPICE PASTES

I am such a huge fan of this kitchen shortcut. When it comes to pulling together a delicious weeknight meal, good quality spice pastes are your friend. In this book I've used a spice paste in my Red Curry Roasted Chicken (pg 72) and also in my Thai Broccoli, Spinach & Coconut Soup (pg 20).

TAHINI

This thick and rich condiment, made from toasted and ground sesame seeds, is the basis of delicious, creamy salad dressings. It's also great in stir fries. I love it on toast drizzled over sliced banana and it can be fantastic in cookies and home baking, such as in muesli bars or bliss balls, especially if nuts and dried fruit are also present. Tahini can separate sometimes and be hard to wrangle but I find lying the jar on its side or upside down, depending on how full it is, allows the oil and solid part to come together again.

TAPIOCA FLOUR

You'll spot tapioca flour (or tapioca starch as it's also called) in some of my recipes. I really like this hardworking gluten free flour because it has a very mild flavour and is so versatile. I use it as a coating on things like my fish tacos, where it creates an excellent crunch. It will do the same thing for chicken or tofu. You cannot use it as a 1:1 substitution for regular flour in baking but it's great as one component in a gluten free flour blend. I like it because it adds a bit of structure to recipes that use a lot of almond meal / ground almonds. I'll use it as the sole flour component in recipes like my Okonomiyaki (pg 104) or my Broccoli & Cheese Fritters (pg 144). It can also be used to thicken sauces. Most supermarkets stock tapioca flour these days, otherwise you will find it in refill stores and organic grocers.

MY FAVOURITE KITCHEN TOOLS

We have a small kitchen and I fiercely guard its limited space, considering any new addition carefully. These are my beloved and most used kitchen tools.

APRON

I LOVE aprons. My essential kitchen armour. I wear one every single time I'm in the kitchen, whether I'm cooking or doing dishes. I'm an enthusiastic (some might say messy) cook and I wouldn't be without one. My favourite are full aprons, with a good-sized pocket and a simple tie at the back (no fussy criss-cross straps).

CAST IRON PANS

These are my kitchen workhorses. I have three cast iron skillets in different sizes that sit on my cooktop, as I use them multiple times every day. Cast iron pans are a pricey kitchen tool but they can last forever when cared for properly (the NZ made ones I own have a hundred year guarantee!).

Once they've been used enough to build up the seasoning, they're very nonstick and they hold heat brilliantly. They'll go from stovetop to oven and also look handsome enough to bring to the table and serve straight from the pan. Ideally you would have different sizes. A smaller one, around 16-18cm, is good for cooking small portions or making sauces. (We don't have a microwave so this is what I use for reheating leftovers.) You'll want a larger pan (26-28cm) for literally everything else.

MICROPLANE

I add citrus zest to dishes constantly and there's nothing better (or quicker) than a microplane for a finely grated zest. You'll also use it for finely shaved Parmesan, ginger or garlic.

MANDOLINE

Owning a mandoline slicer will transform your salads, allowing you to cut beautiful wafer-thin slices of vegetables like radishes and cucumbers. You can quickly cut potatoes and kūmara for gratin and when it comes to slicing cabbage thinly for okonomiyaki, you can do it in no time at all with a mandoline. I prefer a simple handheld one.

SHARP KNIVES

Beautifully sharp knives make your time in the kitchen so much more enjoyable, especially when tackling laborious prep tasks such as dicing lots of onion, celery, carrot and garlic. Sharp knives are safer as they will slip less. I'm not always on top of this but taking the time to sharpen knives at home or have them professionally sharpened is a cooking game changer. Do some research into good brands and build a knife collection slowly. A good first investment knife is a chef knife or Santoku knife. You'll use it for almost everything.

STICK BLENDER

A good stick blender (also called an immersion or hand blender) is a 'must' for making pesto, hummus, salad dressings, mayonnaise, and for blending soups and lots more. For a really reasonable price you can get an appliance that doesn't take up too much room, is easy to clean and you will use again and again. I think they're brilliant. The one I own cost me about $120 and I've had it for 13 years.

STOCK POT

I make broth every week, and having a large saucepan with a lid to make it in is essential. You don't have to buy one that costs the earth and it will last you years and years if you look after it. It will also come in handy when it's time to get into some serious winter batch cooking.

SIMPLE CITRUS JUICER

I use lots of lemon juice in my cooking and it's helpful to have a good little citrus juicer within reach. I like either a wooden handheld juicer, or a traditional glass one with the little surrounding tray and pouring spout. They take up hardly any space and you'll reach for it constantly.

TEA TOWELS

I own and use a LOT of tea towels every day. I feel quite passionate about this kitchen essential. They're so darn handy and I'm liberal with their use. I'm always happy to pull another one from the drawer. I use them for wiping my hands, as a makeshift oven mitt, for extending the draining board surface when I'm hand washing tons of dishes, mopping up spills and, of course, for drying dishes. I'll easily use 5-6 daily when I'm cooking and shooting. You can never own too many.

18 Iceberg Wedge Salad with Tahini Miso Dressing	**28** Black Bean Salad with Coriander & Honey Dressing	**38** Honey & Spice Roasted Vegetable Salad with Honey Tahini Dressing	**50** Everything Soup
20 Thai Broccoli, Spinach & Coconut Soup	**30** Turmeric Roasted Cauliflower with Dates, Pistachios, Mint & Lemon	**40** Chicken Noodle Soup	**52** Hummus & Halloumi Salad
22 New Potato Salad With Crispy Chorizo, Olives, Green Beans & Lemon Mayo	**32** Buckwheat, Silverbeet, Cranberries & Rosemary with Creamy Hummus	**42** Barbecued Vegetable Salad with Chive & Garlic Yoghurt	**54** A Very Simple (& Quite Perfect) Mushroom Soup
24 Puy Lentils & Baby Mozzarella with Basil Dressing & Roasted Cherry Tomatoes	**34** Moroccan Quinoa, Chickpea & Hemp Seed Salad	**44** Grilled Caesar Salad	**56** Everyday Green Salad
26 Red Lentil, Chorizo, Rosemary & Lemon Soup	**36** A Late Spring Vegetable & White Bean Soup	**46** Tortilla Soup	**58** Pork & Quinoa Meatballs With Turmeric Broth
		48 Roasted Vine Tomatoes, Sourdough, Fresh Mozzarella & Green Olives	

Soups
& Salady
Things

ICEBERG WEDGE SALAD WITH TAHINI MISO DRESSING

SERVES 4
GLUTEN FREE | NUT FREE | VEGAN

This is such a simple salad but I absolutely love it. Make sure the lettuce is nice and cold - it's crucial.

1 medium **iceberg lettuce**, chilled

DRESSING
¼ cup **hulled tahini**
1 rounded teaspoon **miso paste** (any will work)
1 teaspoon finely grated **ginger**
1 **garlic clove**, finely chopped
3 tablespoons **lemon** or **lime juice**
¼ cup **water** and more as needed
1 teaspoon **tamari** or **soy sauce**
1 teaspoon **sesame oil**
½ teaspoon **sugar**
Salt and **cracked black pepper** to taste

To garnish: **dukkah** (pg 180), **fried shallots** or **toasted seeds** as desired

Place the dressing ingredients in a small jug and whisk until smooth. Even better, give it a quick whiz with a stick blender as this makes the dressing really creamy.

Remove the outer leaves of the lettuce and cut it into quarters.

Drizzle with the dressing just before serving and garnish with dukkah, fried shallots, toasted seeds or fresh herbs, depending on what you have on hand. All of the toppings suggested will be delicious.

THAI BROCCOLI, SPINACH & COCONUT SOUP

SERVES 4
GLUTEN FREE | NUT FREE | VEGAN

This is a soup I make again and again. It's really delicious, so easy to make and serves up a hefty serving of green goodness.

1 medium **onion**, diced
3 **garlic cloves**, finely diced
4 tablespoons **Thai green curry paste**
2 **medium potatoes**, peeled and cut into small cubes
1 litre **vegetable stock**
1½ cups **water**
2 heads **broccoli**, cut into florets
250g **baby spinach leaves**
1 cup **coconut cream** (a runny variety)
Olive oil for sautéing
Sea salt and **cracked black pepper** to season

To serve: **fresh coriander, crispy shallots**, drizzle of **coconut cream**

Heat a glug of olive oil in a large soup pot over a medium heat. Add the onion and garlic. Cook gently, without browning, for 5 minutes. Add the curry paste and cook for a further minute. Add the potato, stock and water. Bring to a boil and then simmer for 10 minutes. Add the broccoli and simmer for a further 10 minutes. Add the coconut cream and spinach. Cook for 2 minutes before removing from the heat.

Use a blender or stick blender to purée until silky smooth. Season to taste.

NEW POTATO SALAD WITH CRISPY CHORIZO, OLIVES, GREEN BEANS & LEMON MAYO

SERVES 4-6 AS A SIDE
GLUTEN FREE | NUT FREE

It's really nice to add the chorizo to the salad piping hot from the pan, but this isn't essential.

450g **new** or **baby potatoes**
125g **green beans**
Oil for frying
1 **chorizo sausage**
2 cups **salad leaves**
2 **radishes**, sliced thinly
¾ cup **kalamata olives**
Large handful **fresh mint leaves**, roughly chopped
2 tablespoons finely chopped **chives**
Good quality **extra virgin olive** oil for drizzling

LEMON & MUSTARD MAYONNAISE

½ cup **One Minute Mayo** (pg 168) or good quality store-bought **mayonnaise**
1 small **garlic clove**, finely diced
Zest and **juice** of 1 **lemon**
1 teaspoon **wholegrain mustard**

To season: Sea salt and **cracked black pepper**

Place the potatoes in a pot of water, bring to the boil and cook for about 15 minutes or until tender. Drain in a large colander and allow the potatoes to cool to room temperature, or even place in the fridge if prepping ahead of time.

Bring a second pot of water to the boil. Trim the green beans and blanch for 1 minute. Run under very cold water (icy water is even better) and cool as quickly as possible to retain the bright green colour.

Fry the chorizo in a little oil until browned on both sides.

Mix all the dressing ingredients together. Taste and season well.

Scatter the salad leaves on a large plate or platter. Top with the beans and radish slices. Halve the potatoes and arrange on top. Finish with the chorizo, olives and herbs. Drizzle generously with extra virgin olive oil and dollop the lemon & mustard mayonnaise on top.

PUY LENTILS & BABY MOZZARELLA WITH BASIL DRESSING & ROASTED CHERRY TOMATOES

SERVES 4 AS A SIDE
GLUTEN FREE | NUT FREE | VEGETARIAN

A pretty salad that has piles and piles of bright, fresh flavour. On the day I shot this recipe for my book, I served it as part of a meal for friends on a gorgeous summer night. It was fantastic.

250g good quality **cherry tomatoes**, halved
Olive oil for roasting
¾ cup **Puy lentils**
1½ cups **vegetable stock**
Zest of 1 **lemon**
¼ **red onion**, peeled and sliced very thinly
125g **cherry bocconcini** or **fresh mozzarella**, torn in half or into bite-sized pieces
Handful **fresh basil leaves** for salad

DRESSING
¼ cup **olive oil**
1 **garlic clove**, finely diced
Juice of 1 **lemon**
½ teaspoon **sugar**
Large handful **fresh basil leaves** for dressing

To season: Sea salt and **cracked black pepper**

Combine all the dressing ingredients in a small jug or bowl and use a stick blender to blitz until smooth. Set aside until ready to use. Placing it in the fridge for 15 minutes before serving will thicken the dressing a little.

Preheat the oven to 140℃. Place the halved cherry tomatoes in an oven proof dish. Drizzle with olive oil and season with salt and cracked black pepper. Roast for 30 minutes until just starting to shrivel and pucker around the edges. Leave to cool to room temperature.

Place the lentils and stock in a medium saucepan. Bring to the boil. Reduce heat to a low simmer and cook for 15 minutes, with the saucepan lid slightly ajar, until all the liquid has been absorbed and the lentils are tender. Stir through the lemon zest. Leave to cool to room temperature before stirring through the red onion, half the dressing, half the tomatoes and half the fresh basil leaves.

To assemble, spoon the lentils onto a large plate. Scatter over the remaining tomatoes. Scatter over the mozzarella or bocconcini. Drizzle the leftover dressing over the top as desired. Season with a little cracked black pepper and scatter with the remaining fresh basil leaves. Serve immediately.

RED LENTIL, CHORIZO, ROSEMARY & LEMON SOUP

SERVES 6
GLUTEN FREE | NUT FREE

A nourishing family favourite. This one freezes really well and is amazing to have on hand in single portions for lunch. My partner, Luke, loves it with the additional fried chorizo slices on top. It's a nice finishing touch if you've got time.

3 **garlic cloves**, finely diced
1 **brown onion**, diced
1 **chorizo sausage**, sliced thinly
1 teaspoon **smoked paprika**
1 teaspoon **ground cumin**
¼ teaspoon **ground cinnamon**
¼ teaspoon **fennel seeds**
2 teaspoons finely diced **fresh rosemary**
2 cups **split red lentils**
2 litres good quality **vegetable** or **chicken stock**
½ cup **coconut milk**
1 x 400g canned **chopped tomatoes**
Zest of 2 **lemons**
Juice of 1 **lemon**
Olive oil for sautéing
Sea salt and **cracked black pepper**

To serve: **Greek** or **coconut yoghurt**, chopped **chives**, additional **fried chorizo slices**

Heat a generous glug of olive oil in a soup pot over a medium heat. Add the garlic and onions. Sauté until tender and translucent. Add the chorizo and sauté for 3 more minutes.

Add the paprika, cumin, cinnamon, fennel seeds and rosemary. Additional oil can be added if needed. Cook for two minutes before adding the lentils, stock, coconut milk, tomatoes and lemon zest. Bring to the boil and then reduce to a simmer. Cook for around 35 minutes until the lentils are tender and the soup has thickened. Stir through the lemon juice. Taste and season well.

Serve with a dollop of yoghurt on top. Some additional slices of fried chorizo and a drizzle of extra virgin olive oil can be lovely too.

Will last up to five days in an airtight container in the fridge. Can be frozen for up to three months.

BLACK BEAN SALAD WITH CORIANDER & HONEY DRESSING

SERVES 4 AS A SIDE
GLUTEN FREE | NUT FREE | VEGETARIAN

The zingy coriander dressing makes this simple salad really sing.

80g **fresh rocket leaves**
½ **red capsicum**, core removed and sliced thinly
¼ **red onion**, sliced thinly
2 **radishes**, sliced very thinly
½ **avocado**, sliced
100g **creamy feta**
¾ cup cooked **black beans**, well rinsed if from a can
1 cooked **corn cob**, kernels removed or ¾ cup canned **corn kernels**
Handful **cherry tomatoes**, halved
Flaky salt and **cracked black pepper**

DRESSING

Large handful **fresh coriander** or a 50/50 mix **parsley** and **coriander**
⅓ cup good quality **olive oil**
1 rounded teaspoon **honey** or **maple syrup**
Juice of 1 **lemon** or **lime**

Use a stick blender to blitz the dressing ingredients until smooth. Taste and season well.

Select a large plate or platter. Scatter the rocket leaves, capsicum and red onion. Add the radish slices, avocado and crumbled feta. Finish with the black beans, corn and cherry tomatoes.

Drizzle dressing over just before serving and top with a little flaky sea salt and cracked black pepper.

TURMERIC ROASTED CAULIFLOWER WITH DATES, PISTACHIOS, MINT & LEMON

SERVES 4-6 AS A SIDE
GLUTEN FREE | VEGAN

It takes only one pan to create this brilliant, warm salad. Adding the dates and lemon to the hot pan immediately after roasting the cauliflower allows them to soften in the spice-rich oil, and for all the flavours to meld together beautifully.

1 medium head **cauliflower**, cut into florets
1 teaspoon **curry powder**
1 teaspoon **ground turmeric**
Olive oil for roasting
½ **preserved lemon**, finely chopped or **zest** of 1 **lemon**
½ cup **dried dates**, roughly chopped
Large handful **fresh mint**, roughly chopped
¼ cup sliced **spring onion**
½ cup **shelled** and **toasted pistachio nuts**
Sea salt and **cracked black pepper**

Preheat the oven to 220 ℃.

Sprinkle the cauliflower with the curry powder and turmeric. Add a very generous drizzle of olive oil and some sea salt and toss really well to coat evenly.

Roast for around 30 minutes until tender and browned on the tips.

Add the preserved lemon or lemon zest to the hot pan along with the chopped dates, half the mint and half the spring onion. Toss thoroughly. Scatter the pistachio nuts over the top and finish with the remaining herbs. Season with a little flaky sea salt and some cracked black pepper if desired. Serve immediately.

BUCKWHEAT, SILVERBEET, CRANBERRIES & ROSEMARY WITH CREAMY HUMMUS

SERVES 4

GLUTEN FREE | NUT FREE | VEGAN (IF VEGETABLE STOCK IS USED)

Buckwheat is awesome. I really like the subtle grassy flavour. This is such a neat little sautéed side dish or salad. Pair it with other vegetable dishes or any protein.

1¼ cups **raw buckwheat groats**
2½ cups **vegetable** or **chicken stock**
Olive oil for sautéing
1 large **red onion**, diced
3 **garlic cloves**, finely diced
1½ teaspoons finely diced **fresh rosemary leaves**
¼ cup **dried cranberries**
400g **silverbeet leaves**, spines removed and thinly sliced
Juice of 1 **lemon** or more as desired
Toasted pumpkin seeds to garnish
Sea salt and **cracked black pepper**

HUMMUS

1 x 400g canned **chickpeas**, drained and rinsed
2 tablespoons **tahini**
¼ cup **olive oil**
Juice of 1 **lemon**
1 small **garlic clove** (optional)
Water as needed to thin to desired consistency (normally 3-5 tablespoons)

To serve: **toasted pumpkin seeds** to garnish

Rinse buckwheat well using a sieve. Place in a medium saucepan with the stock. Bring to a boil before reducing to a simmer. Cook with a lid just slightly ajar for 15-18 minutes until tender and the liquid has been absorbed. Fluff with a fork. Set aside until needed.

Place all the hummus ingredients into a blender or food processor and blitz until smooth and creamy. A stick blender works well too. Taste and season well.

Heat a generous glug of olive oil in a large sauté pan over a medium heat. Add the onion and cook for 10 minutes, stirring frequently. Add the garlic and cook for another 5 minutes or so until the onion is tender and translucent. Stir the rosemary through and give it a minute in the pan before adding the cranberries and silverbeet. Raise the heat a little higher and cook for a minute or two until the silverbeet has wilted. Add the buckwheat and heat through. Add the lemon juice and a generous seasoning of sea salt and cracked black pepper.

Serve immediately with a dollop of hummus and a sprinkling of toasted pumpkin seeds.

MOROCCAN QUINOA, CHICKPEA & HEMP SEED SALAD

SERVES 6
GLUTEN FREE| VEGAN (IF VEGETABLE STOCK USED)

I've really fallen back in love with quinoa over the last year. Used in the right dishes, its unique texture and flavour is a real delight. This salad can be served warm or cold and is a pleasing mix of flavours. It's fantastic at bbqs, at picnics (it travels well) and alongside most other dishes. I served it on Christmas Day and it was wonderful.

1 cup **quinoa**
2 cups **chicken** or **vegetable stock**
Olive oil for sautéing
1 medium **onion**, diced
3 **garlic cloves**, finely diced
½ teaspoon **fennel seeds**
2 teaspoons **ground cumin**
½ teaspoon **garam masala**
½ teaspoon **smoked paprika**
1 x 400g canned **chickpeas**, drained and rinsed well
Zest of 1 **lemon**
¼ cup **hemp seeds**
Sea salt and **cracked black pepper**
2 medium **carrots**, peeled and cut using a julienne peeler (can also grate)
Juice of 2 **lemons**
6 **dates**, diced
⅓ cup **raw pistachio nuts**, roughly chopped
Large handful **fresh parsley**, roughly chopped
1 tablespoon **fresh thyme leaves**

To serve: **sliced avocado** to top (optional), additional **hemp seeds**, **fresh herbs** to garnish

Place the quinoa and stock in a medium saucepan and bring to the boil. Reduce to a simmer and cook with a lid slightly ajar for 12-15 minutes until tender and the liquid has been absorbed. Remove from heat. Place the lid on tightly and leave to sit for 5 minutes. Remove the lid, fluff up the quinoa with a fork and set aside until ready to use.

Heat a generous glug of oil in a sauté pan over a medium heat. Add the onion and garlic. Cook gently, without browning, for 8-10 minutes until tender and translucent. Add the fennel seeds, cumin, garam masala and smoked paprika. Cook for a further 1 minute, adding additional oil if needed. Add the chickpeas and lemon zest. Cook for another few minutes. Stir through the quinoa and the hemp seeds. Season generously with sea salt and cracked black pepper.

Remove from the heat and leave to cool for 10 minutes before adding the carrot, lemon juice, dates, pistachios, parsley and thyme.

Top with the avocado (if using) just prior to serving. Garnish with extra hemp seeds and fresh herbs.

A LATE SPRING VEGETABLE & WHITE BEAN SOUP

SERVES 4

GLUTEN FREE | NUT FREE | VEGETARIAN (IF USING VEGETABLE STOCK)

Using a flavourful homemade broth will really make this soup shine, but at a pinch a low-salt store-bought stock will work too. This is a simple weeknight soup that I just love. The herbs and lemon zest lift its simple ingredients to become something quite wonderful.

It's essential not to overcook the courgettes and asparagus at the end so that they retain their bright colour and fresh flavour.

Olive oil for sautéing
2 **leeks**, white and very light green part, thinly sliced
3 **garlic cloves**, finely diced
½ teaspoon **dried tarragon**
1 teaspoon **dried thyme**
1 x 400g canned **butter beans**, drained and rinsed
1 x 400g canned **cannellini beans**, drained and rinsed
6 cups **chicken stock,** or homemade **Chicken Broth** (pg 162) or **vegetable stock**
Zest of 1 **lemon**
1 bunch thin **asparagus**, woody end removed, cut into 2cm pieces
2 medium **courgettes**, halved lengthwise and sliced
Sea salt and **cracked black pepper**

To serve: thinly shaved **Parmesan cheese**

Heat a very generous glug of oil in a large saucepan over a medium heat. Add the leeks and a good pinch of salt. Sauté gently, without browning, for 10 minutes. Add the garlic and herbs and cook for a further minute or so. Add the canned beans, stock and lemon zest. Bring to a boil and then simmer for 15 minutes. Add the asparagus and courgettes. Cook for 1 minute.

Remove from the heat. Season generously.

Serve with shaved Parmesan cheese.

HONEY & SPICE ROASTED VEGETABLE SALAD WITH HONEY TAHINI DRESSING

SERVES 4-6 AS A SIDE
GLUTEN FREE | NUT FREE | VEGETARIAN

The gently warmed honey, olive oil and spice marinade gives a glorious flavour boost to these roasted vegetables. Use a flavorful honey for best results. The creamy tahini dressing is absurdly simple, but delicious. I want to pour it on everything.

1 tablespoon **honey**
3 tablespoons **olive oil**
1 rounded teaspoon **ground cumin**
½ teaspoon **smoked paprika**
Generous pinch **chilli flakes** (optional)
½ teaspoon **salt**
2 medium **carrots**, cut into sticks
½ **cauliflower**, cut into florets
1 **red onion**, cut into wedges
1 **red capsicum**, core removed and cut into thick slices
1 x 400g canned **chickpeas**, drained and rinsed well
1 small bunch **asparagus**, trimmed
2 medium **courgettes**, cut into thick diagonal slices
2 **radishes**, cut into wafer-thin slices
Additional **olive oil** as needed for drizzling on asparagus and courgette
Large handful **fresh mint leaves**

HONEY TAHINI DRESSING

1 rounded teaspoon **honey**
2 rounded tablespoons **hulled tahini**
¼ cup **water**
Juice of 1 **lemon**
Sea salt and **cracked black pepper** to taste

Preheat the oven to 220°C.

Place the honey, olive oil, cumin, paprika, chilli flakes (if using) and salt in a small saucepan. Warm gently until the honey is liquid.

Put the carrots, cauliflower, red onion, capsicum and chickpeas in a large bowl. Pour over the marinade and toss well.

Spread out on a large oven tray. Roast for 20-25 minutes. The vegetables should be browned at the edges but not mushy. Toss the asparagus and courgettes in a little olive oil and add to the tray. Roast for a further 5 minutes.

Place all the dressing ingredients in a small jug and use a stick blender (for best results) to blitz until smooth. The dressing should be a good pouring consistency. Taste and season well.

Transfer to a large platter, mixing the radish slices into the salad. Drizzle some of the dressing over the top. Leave the rest to be served on the side and drizzled over individual servings as desired. Scatter the fresh mint on top. Serve immediately.

CHICKEN NOODLE SOUP

SERVES 4
GLUTEN FREE | NUT FREE

This for me, is hands down the best, most comforting, soothing bowl of food you could possibly have. The simple magic of a delicious broth, slurpy noodles and a good dose of vegetables. It's the sort of meal that sets me right when I'm feeling a bit off. Physically or emotionally, it's magic stuff.

Once the broth is made and the chicken cooked (in the broth making process pg 162), the soup itself is a relatively speedy weeknight meal. I like to cook vegetables like the broccolini / broccoli separately (simply pouring boiling water over them) so that the broth flavour stays clean. I only cook the courgettes briefly, letting the hot soup soften them a little before removing from the heat. The aim is for a soup that is delicious and filled with fresh flavour and different textures rather than a soggy, homogeneous bowl. That marriage of a sloooooow cooked broth and quickly cooked vegetables with brightness still intact, is just wonderful.

Enough evangelising from me. Enjoy!

Olive oil for sautéing
1 medium **onion**, diced
2 **garlic cloves**, finely diced
½ stem **celery**, finely diced
1 **carrot**, cut into matchsticks or using a julienne peeler
1.5 litres **chicken stock**, preferably my homemade Chicken Broth (pg 162)
Small handful **fresh dill** or 1 teaspoon **dried dill tips**
1 small bunch **broccolini** or small head **broccoli**, cut into bite-sized pieces
2 medium **courgettes**, sliced on an angle
2 cups (or more) **shredded cooked chicken**
250g **noodles** (I like thick rice noodles)

Sea salt and **cracked black pepper**

For garnishing: additional **fresh dill** (optional)

Heat a glug of olive oil in a large saucepan over a medium heat. Add the onion, garlic and celery and cook gently, without browning, for 12-15 minutes. Add the carrot and cook for 1 minute before adding the stock and dill. Bring to a boil and simmer for 5 minutes.

Place the broccolini in a large bowl and pour boiling water over the top. Leave for 5 minutes before draining and adding to the soup along with the courgettes and chicken. Remove from the heat once it starts bubbling again. Taste and season generously. This will depend on how seasoned the broth was that you started with.

Bring a large pot of water to a boil. Cook the noodles slightly less than the package instructions say (they keep softening in the hot soup). Drain and run under cold water. This stops the noodles from getting gluggy.

Divide the noodles between four bowls. Ladle over the soup, chicken and vegetables. Garnish with additional fresh dill if desired.

BARBECUED VEGETABLE SALAD WITH CHIVE & GARLIC YOGHURT

SERVES 4
GLUTEN FREE | NUT FREE | VEGETARIAN

Eggplant and the other vegetables in this recipe are heavenly when cooked on the bbq. The smoky flavour and charred edges are delicious with the cooling chive and garlic yoghurt.

You'll find me craving this all summer long.

1 medium **eggplant**, sliced into 2cm wide rounds
2 medium **courgettes**, cut into strips
1 **red capsicum**, flesh cut into big chunks
Handful **cherry tomatoes**, halved
Olive oil for brushing on vegetables

CHIVE AND GARLIC YOGHURT
1 cup **Greek style yoghurt**
2 tablespoons finely chopped **chives**
2 **garlic cloves**, finely diced
Zest of 1 **lime** or **lemon**

Sea salt and **cracked black pepper**

To garnish: handful **fresh basil**

Brush the eggplant, courgettes and capsicum generously with olive oil and also sprinkle the eggplant with salt.

Mix together the chive and garlic yoghurt ingredients. Season well. Plenty of cracked black pepper is great in this.

Heat your bbq to a med-high temperature. Cook the courgettes and capsicum until just tender (with lovely grill marks) and the eggplant until very soft. Cut the vegetables into smaller bite-sized pieces.

Spread your large plate or platter with the chive and garlic yoghurt. Layer the barbecued vegetable pieces with the cherry tomatoes and some of the basil leaves. Scatter the remaining basil on top. A sprinkle of flaky salt and a drizzle of extra virgin olive oil is great too.

GRILLED CAESAR SALAD

SERVES 4 AS A SIDE
NUT FREE

I really enjoy a homemade caesar salad. This easy, tasty dressing is best made with good quality mayonnaise, preferably homemade (pg 168).

Charring the lettuce adds a really fabulous smoky flavour. I've used a cast iron skillet but a bbq would work brilliantly as well. Here I forgo the usual addition of bacon because the char of the lettuce and the sprinkle of paprika on the toasty croutons gives enough of a savoury element not to need it. Though by all means, go ahead.

2 thick slices **sourdough** or **other bread**, cut into small chunks
Olive oil for drizzling and grilling
½ teaspoon **smoked paprika**
sea salt
4 free range **eggs**
2 heads **cos lettuce**

DRESSING

1 medium **garlic** clove, diced
5 **anchovies**
½ cup **One Minute Mayo** (pg 168) or good quality store-bought **mayonnaise**
¾ cup finely grated **Parmesan cheese**
Juice of 1 **lemon**
Cracked black pepper

To serve: additional **Parmesan cheese**, thinly shaved.

Preheat the oven to 150°C.

To make the croutons, drizzle the bread with some olive oil, sprinkle with paprika and a generous pinch of sea salt. Toss to coat evenly. Place on a lined baking tray and bake for 20-25 minutes until golden brown.

Make the dressing by placing the garlic and anchovies in a mortar and pestle. Grind together to a smooth paste. Add the rest of the dressing ingredients along with a generous grind of cracked black pepper. Taste and add additional lemon juice or pepper if needed. You could also make this using a stick blender.

Bring a pot of water to a boil. Carefully place the eggs in the water and cook for 6-7 minutes, depending on how cooked you like them (pictured here are size 7 eggs cooked for 6 minutes). Peel and halve.

While the eggs are cooking, cut each head of cos lettuce in half. Heat a dry skillet over a high heat. I like to use my cast iron skillet. Oil it very lightly and cook each lettuce half cut-side down until it is a little charred. This should only take a minute or so.

Serve the charred lettuce drizzled with dressing, then top with croutons and egg. Sprinkle with a little additional Parmesan cheese. A good grind of cracked black pepper is great too.

TORTILLA SOUP

SERVES 4
GLUTEN FREE | NUT FREE | VEGAN
(IF CHEESE OMITTED)

I first ate this when I moved to New York for a few years in my twenties. I was immediately sold on its deliciousness. This is a great easy dinner. We eat it frequently. It's warming and so perfect when you want a punchy mix of flavours and textures. Adding the toppings, so it's just the way you like it, is all part of the fun of eating it. Add some protein in the form of leftover roast chicken, sautéed tofu or prawns if you like.

Olive oil for sautéing
1 medium **onion**, diced
3 **garlic cloves**, finely diced
1 teaspoon **ground cumin**
½ teaspoon **hot smoked paprika**
1 litre **vegetable stock**
2 x 400g cans **chopped tomatoes**
1 x 400g can **black beans**, drained and rinsed
1 x 400g can **chickpeas**, drained and rinsed
¾ cup canned or **frozen corn kernels**
1 tablespoon **lemon** or **lime juice**
Sea salt and **cracked black pepper**

To serve: **corn** chips, sliced **avocado**, **fresh coriander**, **grated cheddar cheese**, **dried chilli flakes** (optional)

Heat a generous glug of olive oil in a soup pot over a medium heat.

Add the onion and garlic. Sauté for 5-10 minutes until the onion is translucent and tender. Add the cumin and paprika and stir through for 1 minute.

Add the stock, tomatoes, beans and chickpeas. Bring to a boil before simmering uncovered for 10 minutes. Add the corn and cook for another minute.

Add the lemon or lime juice, Season well. Divide soup between bowls. Top with corn chips, avocado and coriander. Add dried chilli flakes if you are using them.

Sprinkle over the cheese. Serve immediately.

ROASTED VINE TOMATOES, SOURDOUGH, FRESH MOZZARELLA AND GREEN OLIVES

SERVES 4
NUT FREE | VEGETARIAN

This tray baked warm salad is an absolute delight of textures and temperature. The mozzarella is added right at the end to the hot pan to rest in the wonderful cooking juice from the tomatoes.

I have to confess too, that this is actually the second recipe in the book that pairs tomatoes with mozzarella. What can I say? It's hard to beat.

3 thick slices **sourdough**, torn into chunks
½ cup **chicken** or **vegetable stock**
Extra virgin olive oil
Sea salt and **cracked black pepper**
1 tablespoon **fresh rosemary leaves plus 2 additional short stems**
2 trays **vine tomatoes** (approx. 16 tomatoes)
1 tablespoon **balsamic vinegar**
6 **unpeeled garlic cloves**
250g good quality **fresh mozzarella**
½ cup **Sicilian green olives** (could also use **Kalamata olives**)
Large handful **fresh basil leaves**

Preheat oven to 170℃.

Place the sourdough chunks in a large bowl. Drizzle with the stock and a very generous glug of olive oil. Sprinkle with salt, cracked black pepper and the rosemary leaves. Toss to coat evenly.

Place the tomatoes on a shallow oven proof dish. Drizzle generously with olive oil, the balsamic vinegar and a good seasoning of salt and cracked black pepper. Scatter the sourdough chunks, leaving gaps for where the mozzarella will go at the end. Place the garlic and rosemary stems around the tray. Bake for around 40 minutes until the sourdough has browned and the tomatoes have burst their skins a little and shrivelled slightly. Scatter the olives over the top in the last few minutes of cooking.

Remove the tray from the oven, break the mozzarella into chunks and tuck all around the dish. Finish with the fresh basil on top and serve.

EVERYTHING SOUP

SERVES 6-8
GLUTEN FREE | NUT FREE | VEGAN (IF VEGETABLE STOCK USED)

This hearty soup is full to the brim with goodness. It makes a nice big pot so you'll have plenty of leftovers. There wasn't originally pasta in the recipe but I get such childish pleasure from the addition of some spirals. I especially like using pulse pasta (always cook it separately). I'll often add a bit of protein too. If we're lucky there'll be some leftover roast chicken or some slow-cooked lamb in the fridge. This makes a wonderful addition.

Adapt this recipe as you like and sub in whatever vegetables you have on hand.

Olive oil for sautéing
1 **onion**, diced
4 **garlic cloves**, finely diced
2 medium **carrots**, diced
1 stalk **celery**, diced
1 teaspoon **dried tarragon** (could also use **dried oregano**, **dried mint** or **rosemary**)
1 teaspoon **fennel seeds**
½ teaspoon **ground cinnamon**
¾ cup **red split lentils**
1 large **potato**, washed and cut into small cubes
1 large **kūmara** (purple or orange), peeled and cut into small cubes
2 litres **vegetable**, **chicken** or **beef stock**
2 cups **water**
1 x 400g can **chopped tomatoes**
3 medium **courgettes**, cut into small pieces
250g **greens** (I used chopped frozen kale)
Zest of 1 **lemon**
Juice of ½ **lemon** (or more as needed)
3 tablespoons **soy sauce** or **tamari**
2-3 cups **cooked pasta** (I use red lentil pasta)
Sea salt and **cracked black pepper**

To serve: **extra virgin olive oil** for drizzling, **fresh parsley**

Heat a generous glug of olive oil over a medium heat in a large soup pot. Add the onion, garlic, carrot and celery. Sauté, moving around often, for about 10 minutes until the onion is tender. Add the tarragon, fennel seeds and cinnamon. Cook for a further 1 minute.

Add the lentils, potato, kūmara, stock, water and canned tomatoes. Bring to a boil and then simmer for 30 minutes. Stir regularly.

Add the courgettes, greens, lemon zest, lemon juice and soy sauce. Simmer for a further 5 minutes.

Season to taste.

Ladle the soup into bowls and add half a cup of cooked pasta to each. Drizzle with a little extra virgin olive oil and sprinkle with fresh parsley before serving, if desired.

HUMMUS & HALLOUMI SALAD

SERVES 4
GLUTEN FREE | NUT FREE | VEGETARIAN

Serving a fresh Mediterranean-inspired salad on top of a thick swirl of creamy hummus is a fabulous meal. It's even better with some halloumi piping hot from the pan. Make sure you get a good bit of browning on the halloumi slices. It's the best.

1 **corn cob**
100g mixed **greens** or **rocket leaves**
150g **cherry tomatoes**
2 **radishes**, very thinly sliced
10cm piece **cucumber**, sliced
¼ **red onion**, very thinly sliced
20 **kalamata olives**
1 **avocado**, sliced
Extra virgin olive oil for drizzling
2 **lemons** for drizzling
150g **halloumi cheese**
Sea salt and **cracked black pepper**
Oil for frying

HUMMUS

1 x 400g canned **chickpeas**, drained and rinsed well
4 tablespoons **olive oil**
3 tablespoons **tahini**
3 tablespoons **water** (or more as needed)
Juice of 1 **lemon**

To garnish: thinly sliced **spring onion**, handful **fresh basil leaves**

Combine all the hummus ingredients and use a food processor or a stick blender (my preference) to blitz until smooth and creamy. Add additional water if needed to make it spreadable. Season very generously. Set aside until ready to use.

Bring a saucepan of water to a boil. Cook the corn cob for 3 minutes before draining and rinsing with cold water to cool. Pat dry with a tea towel and use a knife to make vertical slices down the cob. This will make sure the kernels come off in attractive chunks.

Spread 2 large spoonfuls of hummus on one half of each plate (you'll need one plate per person). Scatter the salad greens on the other side. Top with the corn, cherry tomatoes, radishes, cucumber, red onion, olives and avocado

Heat 2 tablespoons of oil in a sauté pan over a medium heat. Cut 1cm slices of halloumi and fry until golden brown on each side. Remove from the pan.

Drizzle each salad with extra virgin olive oil and a squeeze of lemon. Sprinkle with sea salt.

Add the hot halloumi slices to each salad. Scatter generously with the fresh herbs. Serve immediately.

A VERY SIMPLE (& QUITE PERFECT) MUSHROOM SOUP

SERVES 4

GLUTEN FREE | NUT FREE | VEGAN (IF SUGGESTED SUBSTITUTIONS USED)

I find anything with mushrooms irresistible. I love mushroom soup with some crunchy sourdough croutons on top, and maybe also a swirl of homemade Chilli & Garlic Oil (pg 170).

Olive oil for sautéing
1 medium **onion**, diced
3 large **garlic cloves**, finely diced
500g **Swiss brown** or **portobello mushrooms**, sliced
½ teaspoon **dried sage**
½ teaspoon **dried rosemary**
1 medium **potato** (about 250g), peeled and cut into small cubes
1 litre **chicken stock** (use vegetable stock to make vegetarian)
½ cup **cream** (use **coconut milk** to make dairy free)
Sea salt and **cracked black pepper**

Heat a glug of olive oil in a large saucepan over a medium heat. Add the onion and cook for about 10 minutes, until tender and translucent. Add the garlic and cook for another couple of minutes before adding the mushrooms, herbs and a good pinch of salt. Sauté for a few minutes, stirring often until the mushrooms have started to become glassy. Add the potato and stock. Bring to a boil. Simmer for 15 or so minutes. Stir through the cream.

Use a stick blender to purée until very smooth. Season generously.

EVERYDAY GREEN SALAD

SERVES 4 AS A SIDE
GLUTEN FREE | NUT FREE | VEGAN

This barely needs a recipe. A green salad that relies on a simple but delicious dressing, a bed of greens and then a few other fresh elements depending on what's on hand and in season. I love the spicy, crisp bite that radishes bring, with some lightly blanched beans and sweet peas, and firm (not too ripe) avocado. Some toasted seeds would be great here too.

150g **green beans**, trimmed
½ cup **frozen baby peas**
120g mixed **salad leaves**
½ **avocado**, cut into cubes
1-2 **radishes**, thinly sliced
The Dressing for Everything (pg 172)
Flaky salt and **cracked black pepper** to finish (optional)

Place the beans and peas in a large bowl. Cover with boiling water. Leave for 3 minutes. Drain and run under cold water to cool quickly. You can leave them soaking in a bowl filled with cold water and add some ice. Cooling the beans and peas quickly will ensure they retain their bright colour. Drain well once cooled.

Toss the salad leaves with the dressing. Use as much as suits your tastes. Place in a large shallow salad bowl. Top with the beans, peas, avocado and radish slices. Toss lightly. Finish with a little sprinkle of flaky sea salt and cracked black pepper. Serve immediately.

PORK & QUINOA MEATBALLS WITH TURMERIC BROTH

MAKES 20 MEATBALLS - SERVES 4
GLUTEN FREE | NUT FREE

This is such a cosy and flavoursome meal. I'll always turn to a broth-based dinner when I need deep comfort. The meatballs echo the delicious flavour of my favourite dumpling filling in this different format using quinoa.

Homemade chicken broth will again make all the difference here but low-salt store-bought stock will also work. Just check the intensity of flavour. Store-bought stocks can be quite concentrated and you may need to replace 1 cup of stock with water to keep the flavour fresh.

I really hope you make (and love) this recipe.

COOK'S TIP:
To make 1 ½ cups cooked quinoa, place ½ cup of rinsed quinoa with 1 cup water in a small saucepan. Bring to a boil before simmering with a lid slightly ajar for 12-15 minutes until all the liquid has been absorbed. Remove from the heat, place the lid on tightly and leave to sit for 5 minutes. Remove the lid and fluff with a fork. Allow to cool completely before using in this recipe.

PORK AND QUINOA MEATBALLS

400g free range **pork mince**
1½ cups **cooked quinoa** (see cook's tip)
1 free range **egg**
1 **spring onion** (green part), thinly sliced
Handful **fresh coriander**, finely diced
2 **garlic cloves**, finely diced
1 tablespoon finely grated **ginger**
½ teaspoon **ground cumin**
1 teaspoon **sesame oil**
2 tablespoons **soy sauce**
Generous pinch **red chilli flakes** (or as desired)

SOUP BASE

Olive oil for sautéing
½ **onion**, finely diced
2 **garlic cloves**, finely diced
1 teaspoon finely grated **fresh ginger**
1 **carrot**, diced
½ teaspoon **curry powder**
½ teaspoon **ground cumin**
½ teaspoon **ground turmeric**
1 teaspoon **fish sauce**
½ teaspoon **brown sugar**
2 litres **low salt chicken stock** or **homemade Chicken Broth** (pg 162)
2 **baby bok choy**
1 teaspoon **soy sauce** or **tamari**

Seasoning for the broth (as desired): **soy sauce, sesame oil, white pepper, chilli oil**

Place all the meatball ingredients in a bowl and mix really well. Using damp hands, roll into golf ball-sized meatballs. If you've got time, place in the fridge to firm up for 20 minutes.

Heat a glug of oil in a large saucepan over a medium heat. Add the onion and cook for 5-10 minutes until tender and translucent. Add the garlic, ginger and carrot. Cook for a few minutes before adding the curry powder, cumin and turmeric. Allow this to become fragrant in the pan before adding the fish sauce, brown sugar and stock. Bring this to the boil. Reduce to a simmer and cook for 5 minutes, Add the meatballs and bring to the boil again. Reduce to a rapid simmer and cook the meatballs for 5 minutes. Chop the root end from the bok choy and then slice. Add to the soup along with the soy sauce. Allow 1 minute to cook before removing from the heat.

Add additional seasoning to the soup as desired with soy sauce, sesame oil, white pepper and chilli oil.

64
Turmeric & Ginger Lentils

66
Bonnie's Smoky Baked Beans

68
Smash Burgers with The Best Burger Sauce

70
Spiced Fish Tacos with Pickle & Caper Mayo

72
Red Curry Roasted Chicken

74
Spaghetti Aglio Olio E Peperoncino

76
Spanish Style Chicken Tray Bake

78
Greek Cauliflower, Olive & Chickpea Stew

80
Breakfast for Dinner Pizza

82
Mum's Schnitzel

84
Fried Cauliflower Rice with Crispy Fried Eggs

86
Spiced Potato Frittata with Fried Onions, Coriander & Kasundi

88
Soy, Ginger & Sesame Rump Steak

90
Vietnamese Inspired Chicken Lettuce Cups

92
Kimchi Noodles

Simple meals

TURMERIC & GINGER LENTILS

SERVES 4
GLUTEN FREE | NUT FREE | VEGAN

An easy, tasty and economical dish that works for the whole family. A really brilliant one to have in the freezer as a quick dinner to reheat. It's perfect with just some rice and vegetables or as the starting point for the kind of raid-the-fridge bowl dinner I adore. Actually, I love a savoury breakfast with a bit of spice too so I'll also happily have this in the morning with a couple of poached eggs and some avocado on top.

Olive oil or **ghee** for sautéing
1 large **onion**, diced
4 **garlic cloves**, finely diced
2 tablespoons finely grated **ginger root**
1 tablespoon **ground cumin**
1 tablespoon **ground turmeric**
1 teaspoon **ground coriander**
½ teaspoon **smoked paprika**
2 cups **red lentils**
1 x 400g canned **coconut milk**
1 x 400g canned **chopped tomatoes**
3 cups **water**
2 tablespoons **soy sauce** or **tamari**
1 tablespoon **lemon** or **lime juice**
Sea salt and **cracked black pepper**

To serve: **plain yoghurt** or **coconut yoghurt**, **fresh coriander**

Heat a generous glug of oil in a large pot over a medium-low heat. Cook the onion until tender and translucent. Add the garlic and ginger and cook for a further minute or so. Add the spices. Give these a minute or two in the pan to become fragrant. Add a splash of oil if the pan is dry.

Add the lentils, coconut milk, tomatoes, water and soy sauce. Bring to a boil and then simmer for 20-25 minutes until the lentils are tender and the texture is thickened. Add the lemon juice and season (generously) to taste.

COOK'S TIP
I'll often throw some fresh or frozen spinach in here in the last few minutes of cooking. Peas are another good way to make this go further.

If you have a little bit of this left over you can create a quick soup by thinning it out with some stock and a squeeze of lemon juice, and adding pan-fried tofu or roasted cauliflower (or both!) and toasted seeds.

BONNIE'S SMOKY BAKED BEANS

SERVES 4
GLUTEN FREE | NUT FREE | VEGAN

I taught my eldest daughter Bonnie how to make this when she was nine, because she loves hearty bean dishes. It's really simple to prepare and is fantastic alongside eggs at brunch, in a bowl with chunks of sourdough to dip in it, or with sausages for a cosy meal. Adding a can of corn kernels or corn from a fresh cob is great too. Add them in the last few minutes of cooking to keep their sweetness.

Olive oil for sautéing
2 medium **onions**, diced
4 **garlic cloves**, finely diced
2 teaspoons **ground cumin**
½ teaspoon **ground coriander**
½ teaspoon **garam masala**
1 teaspoon **smoked paprika**
Pinch **dried chilli flakes** (plus more if desired)
2 x 400g cans **chopped tomatoes**
1½ cups **water**
1 x 400g canned **cannellini beans**, drained and rinsed
1 x 400g canned **black beans**, drained and rinsed
1 x 400g canned **butter beans**, drained and rinsed
1 tablespoon **tamari** or **soy sauce**
Sea salt and **cracked black pepper**

Heat a generous glug of oil in a sauté pan over a medium heat. Add the onions and cook until translucent and tender. Add the garlic and cook, moving frequently, for a further minute. Add the spices and give them a minute in the pan to become fragrant. Add the remaining ingredients and bring to a boil.

Reduce to a simmer and cook for 25-30 minutes until the sauce has reduced and thickened, stirring often to prevent it sticking to the bottom of the pan. Add more water if the sauce has dried up too much. Season well.

Can be stored in the fridge in an airtight container for up to four days. Will freeze brilliantly for up to six months.

SMASH BURGERS WITH THE BEST BURGER SAUCE

SERVES 4
NUT FREE

This is the only way to make burger patties. It's SO easy. Don't be tempted to form proper patties with the beef mince. It's the rough portions of meat on the searing hot pan that guarantee loads of delicious caramelised bits - the tell-tale sign of a perfect smash burger. My recipe makes a double patty burger for extra decadence. The burger sauce is an absolute must-do. It's perfect for dipping your fries too.

800g **beef mince**
Sea salt and **cracked black pepper**
8 slices **cheese**
Olive oil for cooking

BURGER SAUCE

½ cup **One Minute Mayo** (pg 168) or good quality store-bought **mayonnaise**
10 sliced **pickles**, diced (I like a sweet and spicy pickle)
1 tablespoon **pickle brine**
2 teaspoons **American style mustard**
1 tablespoon **tomato sauce** or **ketchup**
½ teaspoon **garlic powder**
½ teaspoon **onion powder**
½ teaspoon **smoked paprika**
Generous pinch **salt**

To serve: toasted **brioche buns**, **lettuce**, sliced **tomatoes**, sliced **red onion**, extra slices of **pickles**

Mix together all the sauce ingredients and place in the fridge for at least 30 minutes for the flavours to develop.

Divide the mince with a knife or a large spoon into 8 roughly equal portions. It doesn't have to be precise or tidy. Heat a pan (a cast iron pan is perfect) or a bbq hot plate until very hot. Lightly oil the pan. Place portions of meat in the pan as space allows, trying not to overcrowd the pan. Use a metal spatula and press down very firmly to flatten right down. Season generously with sea salt and cracked black pepper. Wait until you can see the meat browning really well at the edges before flipping it over - usually a minute or two. Place a slice of cheese on that cooked side and cook for a further minute or so until done to your liking.

Butter the toasted buns. Spread the top bun with the burger sauce. Place lettuce leaves and sliced tomatoes on the bottom bun. Top with two burger patties. Finish with sliced red onion and extra pickles.

SPICED FISH TACOS WITH PICKLE & CAPER MAYO

SERVES 4
GLUTEN FREE | NUT FREE

Happiness is a freshly cooked fish taco. Enjoy with your favourite people and some cold drinks.

½ cup **tapioca** or **potato flour**
1 teaspoon **curry powder**
¼ teaspoon **smoked paprika**
½ teaspoon **sea salt**
Cracked black pepper
600g **firm white fish**
Oil for frying

PICKLE & CAPER MAYO

½ cup **One Minute Mayo** (pg 168) or good quality store-bought **mayonnaise**
2 tablespoons **capers**
½ teaspoon **dried dill**
10 slices good quality **pickles**, diced (I like a slightly sweet variety for this)
Zest of 1 **lime**
2 teaspoons **lime juice**
Sea salt and **cracked black pepper**

TO ASSEMBLE

Soft corn tortillas
Finely shredded cabbage (a mix of red and green is ideal)
1 **avocado**, sliced thinly
2 **radishes**, sliced thinly
Handful **fresh coriander**, roughly chopped
Lime wedges

Combine the Pickle & Caper Mayo ingredients in a small bowl and stir well. Check seasoning and adjust as desired. Place in the fridge until ready to use.

Combine the flour, curry powder, paprika, salt and pepper in a large bowl. Stir well.

Cut the fish into bite-sized pieces and toss in the seasoned flour to coat.

Heat 1.5cm of oil in a sauté pan over a medium-high heat. Cook the fish in 2 batches (to avoid overcrowding the pan) until golden and crunchy. A minute or so on each side should be plenty.

To assemble

Heat the tortillas. Top each with a small handful of shredded cabbage, 1-2 slices of avocado and some radish slices. Place a few pieces of fish on each, drizzle with the pickle and caper mayo and garnish with coriander. Serve immediately.

RED CURRY ROASTED CHICKEN

SERVES 4
GLUTEN FREE | NUT FREE

Using store-bought spice paste is a brilliant shortcut to creating a dinner that is utterly delicious. I love serving this chicken with rice noodles and steamed greens. It's also fabulous with cauliflower rice or konjac noodles. I really like to use a butterflied chicken for this dish so as much chicken as possible is in contact with the rich cooking liquid, but if you don't feel confident cutting your chicken in this way don't worry, just be sure to baste a few extra times during cooking.

1 medium sized free range **chicken**, ideally butterflied
120g **red curry paste**
1 x 400g canned **coconut milk**
¾ cup **chicken stock**
Zest and **juice** of 1 **lime**

To garnish (optional): finely sliced **spring onion**, **fresh coriander leaves**, **lime wedges**

Preheat the oven to 180°C.

Place the chicken in an oven proof dish with high sides.

Whisk together the curry paste, coconut milk, chicken stock, lime juice and zest. Pour this over the chicken. Roast the chicken for 1½ hours (more if your chicken is not butterflied) or until the juices run clear when cut at the thickest part of the thigh. Baste at least 4 times with the liquid during the cooking process.

SPAGHETTI AGLIO OLIO E PEPERONCINO

SERVES 4
VEGAN (IF PARMESAN OMITTED) | NUT FREE

My girls call this Dad's pasta. It's Luke's specialty; an easy Sunday night dinner that we all love. The entire dish hinges on using excellent, full flavoured olive oil. The well salted pasta water means you won't need any other added salt. Though not traditional, we like ours with a scattering of Parmesan cheese.

We always have a really lemony rocket salad on the side.

400g good quality **spaghetti**
½ cup **extra virgin olive oil**
4 **garlic cloves**, finely diced
½-1 teaspoon **dried chilli flakes** (according to taste)
Handful **fresh parsley**, roughly chopped
1 tablespoon **salt** to season pasta water

To serve: **cracked black pepper**, finely grated **Parmesan cheese** (if desired)

Bring a large pot of water to a boil. Add the salt to the water. Add the pasta and cook for 1-2 minutes less than the packet instructions. Meanwhile, place the oil and garlic in a sauté pan over a medium heat. Cook the garlic very gently for a couple of minutes. Add a good ladle of the starchy pasta water. This is great for letting the garlic continue cooking without burning. Stir constantly, letting the water and oil emulsify a little and become a "sauce". Add the drained pasta and toss well. Add in the dried chilli flakes and parsley and cook for a minute or so. Divide between 4 bowls. Add some finely grated Parmesan cheese if desired.

SPANISH STYLE CHICKEN TRAY BAKE

SERVES 4
GLUTEN FREE | NUT FREE

I love a tray bake. It looks so lovely being brought to the table and served directly from the dish. This one is an absolute delight.

600g **baby potatoes**
Olive oil for roasting
1 **red capsicum**, sliced
1 **red onion**, cut into wedges
200g **cherry tomatoes**, halved
2 tablespoons **olive oil** for marinating chicken
1 teaspoon **smoked paprika**
¼ teaspoon **ground cinnamon**
Zest of 1 **lemon**
1 teaspoon **sea salt**
Cracked black pepper
Generous pinch **chilli flakes** (optional)
6 free range **boneless chicken thighs**
Small handful **thyme sprigs**
½ cup **pitted olives** (use black, green or kalamata)

Preheat the oven to 200°C.

Halve any larger potatoes. The smaller ones can be left whole. Place in a pot of water and bring to a boil. Simmer for 10 minutes. Drain well.

Place the potatoes in the large oven proof dish you'll be cooking the whole meal in. Drizzle generously with olive oil and season well. Roast for 20 minutes.

Add the capsicum, onion and cherry tomatoes to the tray. Add additional oil and salt and toss well.

Mix together the 2 tablespoons of olive oil, paprika, cinnamon, lemon zest, salt and pepper. Add chilli flakes if using. Add the chicken and toss until well coated. Put the chicken thigh fillets on top of the vegetables, tucking the ends underneath.

Place thyme sprigs over the top, pop in the oven and roast for 35-40 minutes until the chicken is golden and the vegetables are tender. Scatter the olives on top in the last 5 minutes.

Serve immediately with fresh parsley sprinkled over and lemon wedges on the side if desired.

GREEK CAULIFLOWER, OLIVE & CHICKPEA STEW

SERVES 6
GLUTEN FREE | NUT FREE | VEGAN
(IF FETA OMITTED)

A hearty and super tasty vegetarian main that can easily stand on its own, but will also be perfect for a shared feast or with any protein you enjoy.

This could be served with steamed rice or quinoa on the side. Crusty bread is also delicious.

1 medium head **cauliflower**
Olive oil for roasting and sautéing
1 medium **onion**, diced
4 large **garlic cloves**, finely diced
1 large **carrot**, diced
2 stems **celery**, thinly sliced
2 teaspoons **dried oregano**
½ teaspoon **ground cinnamon**
3 x 400g cans **chopped tomatoes**
2½ cups **vegetable stock**
1 x 400g canned **chickpeas**, drained and rinsed well
24 **pitted kalamata olives** (approximately)
Large handful **fresh parsley**, roughly chopped
120g **feta cheese** (or more if desired), roughly crumbled
Sea salt and **cracked black pepper**

Preheat the oven to 200°C.

Cut the cauliflower into florets and discard the core. Place on an oven proof tray. Drizzle generously with olive oil and roast for 30 minutes. Set aside until ready to use.

Heat a good glug of oil in a large sauté pan over a medium heat. Add the onion, garlic, carrot and celery. Cook without browning (lower heat if necessary) until the onion is tender. Add the oregano and cinnamon. Cook for a further two minutes.

Add the canned tomatoes and stock. Bring to a boil, before reducing to a simmer. Cook for 20 minutes until the sauce has thickened and is glossy. Add the chickpeas and olives. Cook for a further 10 minutes. Add the cauliflower. Cook for 5 minutes. Stir through half the parsley and half the feta cheese. Season well with sea salt and cracked black pepper.

Scatter the remaining parsley and feta cheese on top.

BREAKFAST FOR DINNER PIZZA

MAKES 1 PIZZA / SERVES 2
GLUTEN FREE (IF GF BASE USED) } NUT FREE

I will happily eat these favourite breakfast flavours at any time of day.

1 store bought **pizza base** or my One Bowl Gluten Free Pizza Base (pg 178)
½ cup **tomato passata** or **purée**
1 cup grated **mozzarella cheese**
¼ **red onion**, thinly sliced
4 (or more) slices **smoked salmon**
6 **cherry tomatoes**, halved
1 tablespoon **capers**, drained
1 free range **egg**
½ an **avocado**, sliced
Small handful **wild rocket leaves**

To garnish: **flaky sea salt, cracked black pepper, dried chilli flakes** as desired

Preheat the oven to 220°C.

Spread the pizza base with the tomato passata. Sprinkle the cheese and red onion on top. Arrange the smoked salmon slices over this. Add the cherry tomatoes (cut side up) and capers.

Crack the egg on top in the middle of the pizza.

Bake for 8-12 minutes until the cheese is lightly golden.

Slice the avocado and arrange on top of the pizza once it is cooked. Scatter over the rocket leaves. Finish with flaky salt, cracked black pepper and dried chilli flakes as desired.

Serve immediately.

MUM'S SCHNITZEL

SERVES 4
NUT FREE

Occasionally there's a meal so steeped in happy nostalgia for me, that it can only be done one way. My mum and my grandmother both made their schnitzel crumbed in store-bought sage and onion stuffing mix. It's a super tasty shortcut. With a crunchy, coarse crumb and dried herbs in there to give it a yummy flavour. This was always my requested birthday meal growing up and my kids absolutely love it now. Luke teased me a bit for putting this in the book but I was adamant. Enjoy with a giant green salad.

A meat mallet or tenderiser makes all the difference in getting a uniform thickness to your chicken and it will make the meat super tender. It's such a handy kitchen tool.

600g free range **chicken breasts**
200g store-bought **sage and onion stuffing mix**
2-3 free range **eggs**
Oil for frying

If the chicken breasts are large, cut them in half through the middle to create thinner pieces.

Lay a piece of baking paper over the top and pound until the pieces are around 1 cm thick.

You can cut these big pieces smaller if you like (for children perhaps).

Spread the stuffing mix out on a large plate and whisk the eggs in a shallow bowl. Have another plate ready for your finished schnitzel.

Coat each piece of chicken in egg and then coat really well in the stuffing mix. Repeat until all the chicken is coated in crumbs.

Heat 1.5cm of oil in a skillet over medium heat. Cook the schnitzel in batches for 2-3 minutes until golden on each side and cooked through. Place in a warm oven until you've finished cooking.

Serve with a big green salad.

FRIED CAULIFLOWER RICE WITH CRISPY FRIED EGGS

SERVES 4
GLUTEN FREE | VEGAN (IF EGG OMITTED)

The poor old cauli has been contorted in all sorts of mad ways in the name of health over the last decade. Some of it's well outside the level of effort I'm willing to exert regularly (I'm looking at you, cauliflower pizza base), but this dish, using cauliflower rice, is fantastic. It's really tasty and I've been making it for years. A quick meal (once you've chopped the cauli) and the flavour is fab.

Store-bought cauliflower rice is convenient but is often pretty waterlogged even after cooking. Make your own at home in a food processor if possible.

½ large **cauliflower**
Oil for sautéing
1 **onion**, diced
2 **garlic cloves**, finely diced.
1 heaped teaspoon finely diced **ginger**
1 **carrot**, peeled and chopped into small cubes
½ cup **frozen peas**
¾ cup **roasted cashew nuts**
1 tablespoon **tamari** or **soy sauce**
1 **spring onion**, thinly sliced
1 teaspoon **toasted sesame oil**
4 free range **eggs** (one per person)

To serve: additional **spring onion, sesame seeds, dried chilli flakes**

Cut cauliflower into large chunks. Place in a food processor and blitz until it has a rice-like texture. You may need to do it in two batches depending on the size of your machine.

Heat a generous glug of oil in a sauté pan over a medium heat. Add onion, garlic, ginger and carrot. Cook until the onion is tender and transparent. Push to the side of the pan. Add a little more oil and turn the heat up. Add the cauliflower rice and fry for a minute without moving (this bit of browning adds flavour). Mix it all back together again and cook for approximately five minutes until the cauliflower rice is tender but not gluggy. Add the peas, cashew nuts, tamari and spring onion. Mix well. Taste and add additional seasoning if desired.

Take off the heat. Drizzle with sesame oil and toss well. Set aside while the eggs cook.

Heat a good spoonful of oil over a medium-high heat in a sauté pan. Carefully break the eggs into the pan and cook until the whites are crispy at the edges and the yolk is cooked to your liking.

Divide the cauliflower rice between four plates. Top each with a fried egg. Garnish with additional spring onions, some sesame seeds and dried chilli flakes as desired.

SPICED POTATO FRITTATA WITH FRIED ONIONS, CORIANDER & KASUNDI

SERVES 4
GLUTEN FREE | NUT FREE | VEGETARIAN

An eggy dinner can really save the day when the cupboards are a bit bare. This one is delicious both hot and cold. I love a really good tomato kasundi dolloped on top just before it goes in the oven, but any good relish you have on hand will work.

450-500g **potatoes**, in bite-sized pieces
Olive oil for sautéing
2 medium **onions**, diced
2 **garlic cloves**, finely diced
1½ teaspoons **curry powder**
8 free range **eggs**
½ cup **cream**
Large handful **coriander leaves**, roughly chopped
1 **spring onion**, green part thinly sliced
Sea salt and **cracked black pepper**
8 **cherry tomatoes**, halved
Tomato kasundi or other **relish** to dollop on top

Preheat oven to 200℃.

Place the potatoes in a medium saucepan filled with water and bring to a boil. Simmer for 15-20 minutes or until potatoes are tender (but not mushy). Drain in a colander. Leave in the colander to cool and dry out.

Heat a generous glug of oil in a sauté pan over medium heat. Cook the onion for 10 minutes until translucent and tender. Add the garlic and cook for a further minute. Add the curry powder and allow a minute in the pan to become fragrant. Remove from the heat.

Whisk together the eggs, cream, coriander, spring onion and the curried onion and garlic. Add a generous pinch of salt and a good grind of black pepper. Mix well.

Grease a 28cm oven proof dish (I use a cast iron skillet). Pour in the egg mixture. Add the potatoes and spread out evenly. Top with the cherry tomatoes (cut side up) and then place dollops of kasundi or any other relish you enjoy on top.

Bake for roughly 30-35 minutes until golden brown and set.

SOY, GINGER & SESAME RUMP STEAK

SERVES 4
GLUTEN FREE | NUT FREE

An inexpensive cut of steak becomes something very delicious (and requested often) when given some time in this crowd-pleasing marinade, and then cooked on the bbq to smoky perfection. Do not overcook your steak! This is so important, especially when serving it to kids. Well rested, juicy, tender meat will inspire an enjoyment of steak, while dry and overcooked meat will chase them away forever.

Allow the steak 5-10 minutes to rest after cooking and then slice thinly. I always serve steak sliced for sharing at our table. It makes the meat go further and I think the presentation is more inviting this way.

¼ cup **soy sauce** or **tamari**
1 teaspoon **toasted sesame oil**
1 teaspoon **honey**
1 tablespoon finely grated **ginger root**
2 **garlic cloves**, finely diced
White pepper
500-600g **rump steak**

To serve: thinly sliced **spring onions**, **crispy shallots**

Whisk together the soy sauce, sesame oil, honey, ginger and garlic. Add a good seasoning of white pepper. Place this in a shallow bowl and add the steak, coating well on each side. Leave the steak to marinate in the fridge for up to 8 hours. Turn a few times to ensure it's well coated.

Cook on a preheated bbq, over a medium-high temperature for approximately 2-2½ minutes on each side. This will depend a little on your bbq and the thickness of the meat. Rest for 5-10 minutes under a very loose piece of foil. Reserve any juices that collect in the resting dish. Slice thinly and serve with a sprinkling of crispy shallots and thinly sliced spring onions. Drizzle with the resting juices and serve immediately.

VIETNAMESE INSPIRED CHICKEN LETTUCE CUPS

SERVES 4
GLUTEN FREE | NUT FREE

A brilliant way to use up leftover roast chicken. You could also just grab a cooked free range chicken from the supermarket and you've got a super easy (very delicious) weeknight meal.

150g **vermicelli noodles**
3 cups (roughly) **shredded chicken**
Handful **fresh mint leaves**, thinly sliced

DRESSING

3 tablespoons **lime juice**
2 tablespoons **fish sauce**
2 tablespoons **water**
1 teaspoon **sesame oil**
4 teaspoons **brown sugar**
½-1 **red chilli**, deseeded and diced

TO ASSEMBLE

Cos lettuce or baby gem lettuce leaves, washed
Grated carrot
Cucumber, cut into matchsticks
Crispy shallots
Additional fresh mint leaves to garnish

Combine all the dressing ingredients in a small jug and whisk together.

Place the vermicelli in a bowl and cover with boiling water for 5 minutes.

Rinse under cold water and drain.

Combine the chicken, noodles, mint and ¾ of the dressing and toss together well.

Serve generous spoonfuls of the chicken and noodles in the lettuce leaves. Add grated carrot and cucumber as desired and drizzle with a little more of the dressing. Garnish with crispy shallots.

KIMCHI NOODLES

SERVES 4
GLUTEN FREE | NUT FREE | VEGETARIAN

The delicious, bold flavour of kimchi is perfect for creating a speedy weeknight noodle dish.

200g **dried thick rice noodles** (pad thai noodles)
Oil for sautéing
½ **onion**, diced
2 large **garlic cloves**, finely diced
1 tablespoon **finely grated ginger root**
1 **red chilli**, seeds removed and diced
1 **carrot**, grated or julienned
½ cup **frozen peas**
1 large **head broccoli**, cut into florets
2 tablespoons **tamari**
½–¾ cup **kimchi**, roughly chopped
2 free range **eggs**, lightly whisked
1 teaspoon **toasted sesame oil**
Handful **fresh coriander**, roughly chopped

To garnish: **sesame seeds**

Cook noodles in a large pot of boiling water according to packet instructions. Drain and rinse well in cold water. Set aside until needed.

Heat a generous glug of oil in a large sauté pan over a medium heat. Add the onion and cook until translucent. Add the garlic, ginger and chilli and cook for another minute or so. Raise the heat slightly and add the carrot, peas and broccoli. Cook for five minutes until the broccoli is just cooked. Mix through the noodles, tamari and the kimchi. Sauté for 2 minutes until hot. Make a big space in the middle of the hot noodles. Add the eggs. Allow to sit for a minute in the hot pan before tossing through the noodles. Cook for 1 minute further before removing from the heat. Toss through the sesame oil and coriander.

Serve immediately topped with sesame seeds.

98
Kedgeree with Smoked Salmon & Dill

100
Chicken, Mushroom & Black Pepper Wonton Soup

102
Kelly's Fish Pie

104
Okonomiyaki

106
Moroccan Lamb Lasagne with Cauliflower Béchamel

108
Beef & Mushroom Stew with Cheddar & Parsley Dumplings

110
Mexican Spiced Beef Cheeks with Coriander & Jalapeno Sauce

112
Creamy Chicken, Chickpea & Spinach Curry

114
Rich Mushroom & French Lentil Pie with Crunchy Filo Topping

116
Green Risotto

118
Roast Chicken & Sourdough

120
Spiced Slow Roasted Lamb Leg with Fresh Herb Sauce & Pomegranate Seeds

122
Vegan Tray Bake Nachos with Tofu, Mushroom & Lentil Chilli

124
Broccoli & Greens Tart with Buckwheat & Brown Rice Crust

Slightly More Effort (but worth it)

KEDGEREE WITH SMOKED SALMON & DILL

SERVES 4-6
GLUTEN FREE | NUT FREE

This is one of those dishes that if you love it, you usually really LOVE it. I grew up eating kedgeree and for me, it's nostalgia and comfort all rolled into one. I've used New Zealand hot smoked salmon because I enjoy its bright colour and richness but use whatever smoked fish you favour. Traditionally eaten as a breakfast or brunch dish, it also makes a fab supper or weekend lunch.

50g **butter**
1 **brown onion**, diced
3 **garlic cloves**, finely diced
1 large **red chilli**, deseeded and finely diced
1 rounded teaspoon finely grated **ginger root**
2 teaspoons **curry powder**
1 teaspoon **ground turmeric**
¼ teaspoon **ground cinnamon**
1½ cups **basmati rice**
750ml **chicken stock**
1 **bay leaf**
4 free range **eggs**
200g fillet **hot smoked salmon** (or whatever smoked fish you enjoy)
Handful **fresh dill**, roughly chopped
2 tablespoon thinly sliced **chives**
1 **spring onion**, thinly sliced
Flaky sea salt and **cracked black pepper** to season

To garnish: additional **fresh herbs**

Heat the butter in a large saucepan over a medium heat. Add the onion and cook for 10 minutes until tender and translucent. Add the garlic, chilli and ginger. Cook for a further few minutes. Add the spices and give these a minute in the pan to become fragrant.

Add the rice and stir well to coat in the butter and spices.

Pour in the chicken stock and add the bay leaf. Bring to a boil, before reducing the heat to low and cooking with a lid very slightly ajar for around 12 minutes or until all the liquid has been absorbed. Place the lid on tightly, remove from the heat and leave to stand for 5 minutes. Fluff with a fork.

Bring a pot of water to a boil. Add the eggs and cook for 7 minutes. Run under cold water and peel.

Remove any skin from the smoked salmon and break into bite-sized pieces.

Carefully toss the smoked salmon and the herbs through the rice. Quarter the eggs, nestle them into the rice (I prefer this to tossing them through and breaking the eggs apart) and scatter the remaining herbs on top.

Finish with some flaky sea salt and a good grind of cracked black pepper.

CHICKEN, MUSHROOM & BLACK PEPPER WONTON SOUP

SERVES 4 GENEROUSLY (WITH PLENTY OF WONTONS LEFT OVER)
DAIRY FREE

I loooooove homemade wonton soup. My daughter Bonnie and I especially look forward to it. Tender, flavoursome parcels in a tasty broth, it's absolute perfection to me.

We always serve it with homemade chilli oil (pg 170).

Folding the wontons is surprisingly easy and rather enjoyable.

400g free range **chicken mince** (could also use free range pork)

150g **Swiss brown** or **small Portobello mushrooms**, diced

2 teaspoons finely grated **ginger**

1 large **garlic clove**, finely diced

1 **spring onion**, green part finely sliced

2 teaspoons **toasted sesame oil**

2 teaspoons **soy sauce**

½ teaspoon **finely ground black pepper**

1 packet **wonton wrappers** (you'll need about 50)

BROTH

Oil for sautéing

1 **garlic clove**, finely diced

2 rounded teaspoons **ground ginger**

6 cups **low salt chicken stock** (homemade Chicken Broth is ideal, pg 162)

1 teaspoon **toasted sesame oil**

2 teaspoons **rice wine vinegar** or **Chinese black vinegar**

1 teaspoon **sugar** (any kind is fine)

2 teaspoons **soy sauce** (plus more to taste as desired)

2 heads **baby pak choy**, halved or quartered

Wonton method

Combine the mince, mushrooms, ginger, garlic, spring onion, sesame oil, soy sauce and black pepper. Mix together well.

Lay out some wonton wrappers – usually 6 at a time is good – and put a small dish of water close by. Place around a teaspoon of filling in the middle of the wrapper. Dip your finger in the water and lightly wet around the edge of the wrapper. Fold in half to create a rectangle and use your fingers to press the folded wrapper together to create a tight seal. Bring the two bottom corners together and pinch to join.

Place the finished wontons on a plate lined with baking paper to prevent sticking. Repeat this process until all your filling is used. Place in the fridge until ready to use.

Broth method

Heat a glug of oil in a large pot over a medium low heat. Cook the garlic and ginger gently for a few minutes. Add the chicken stock, sesame oil, rice wine vinegar, sugar and soy sauce. Bring to a boil.

Simultaneously bring another large pot of water to a boil to cook the wontons.

Drop as many wontons as you'd like to serve into the boiling water. Around 6-8 per person is a good starting point. Gently stir the water into a whirlpool when the wontons first enter the water to prevent them sticking to the bottom.

Cook for 4 minutes before lifting wontons out with a slotted spoon and dropping them into the soup to cook for a further minute. Add the halved pak choy at this point too and let it simmer for a minute along with the wontons.

Divide the soup and wontons between the bowls. Garnish with toasted sesame seeds, sliced spring onion and chilli oil.

COOK'S TIP
Folded raw wontons can be frozen for later use. Simply freeze in a single layer on a plate lined with baking paper. Once the wontons are frozen you can pop them into freezer bags until needed. Can be cooked from frozen. Simply boil for 2 minutes longer.

KELLY'S FISH PIE

SERVES 4-6
NUT FREE

I make this every Easter, and then as many other times as possible throughout the year. Yummy with a crisp glass of chardonnay.

Olive oil for sautéing
1 medium **onion**, diced
2 large **garlic cloves**, finely diced
50g **butter**
⅓ cup **flour**
750mls **milk**
3 tablespoons **capers**, drained
1 teaspoon **grainy mustard**
Handful **fresh parsley**, roughly chopped
Handful **fresh dill**, roughly chopped
Zest of 1 **lemon**
300g **smoked fish**, bones and skin discarded
300g **firm white fish**, cut into bite-sized pieces
3 free range **eggs**, hard-boiled and peeled
3 cups **mashed potato**
1 cup **panko bread crumbs**
Butter for topping
Sea salt and **cracked black pepper**

Preheat the oven to 200°C.

Heat a generous glug of olive oil in a saucepan over a medium heat. Add the onion and cook until tender and translucent. Add the garlic and cook for a further minute. Add the butter and let it melt before adding the flour and mixing well. Cook the butter and flour for 1-2 minutes without browning. Add the milk in stages and whisk continuously to eliminate any lumps. Bring to a boil and then simmer for 3-5 minutes more until the sauce is nicely thickened.

Add the capers, mustard, parsley, dill and lemon zest. Season with salt and pepper. Mix well. Remove from the heat.

Break the smoked fish into bite-sized pieces and fold through the sauce along with the fresh fish. Spoon into an oven proof dish. Cut the hard boiled eggs into quarters and scatter over the top.

Top with the mashed potato and then the bread crumbs. Dot some butter over the top to make the breadcrumbs crunchy and golden.

Bake for roughly 30-35 minutes or until the top is golden brown and the sauce is bubbling hot.

Leave to sit for 10 minutes before serving.

OKONOMIYAKI

SERVES 4 – MAKES 8 MEDIUM SIZED PANCAKES

GLUTEN FREE | NUT FREE | VEGETARIAN (IF FISH SAUCE AND BONITO FLAKES OMITTED)

My version of this Japanese street food is a casual family dinner we love. Even when the cupboards feel pretty bare, I'll usually have the bits and pieces needed to make this recipe. I like to cram in lots of vegetables. The simple ingredients yield such a delicious result. The fish sauce (in the mixture) and bonito flakes (as a topping) are really lovely elements for flavour but can be left out to make this dish vegetarian.

I tend to use my homemade One Minute Mayo (pg 168) as one of the toppings. Popping it in a little squeezy bottle makes it a bit more fun when dressing the okonomiyaki. In the absence of proper okonomiyaki sauce I use a not-too-sweet barbecue sauce.

½ medium **cabbage**
2 large **kale leaves**
1 medium **carrot**
5 free range **eggs**, lightly whisked
1 **spring onion**, sliced thinly
1 tablespoon finely grated **ginger root**
1½ tablespoons **fish sauce** (omit if vegetarian)
2 tablespoons **soy sauce** or **tamari**
1¼ cups **tapioca starch** or **white rice flour**
1 teaspoon **baking powder**
Oil for frying

To serve: additional sliced **spring onion**, grated **radish**, **bbq sauce** or **mayonnaise**, **bonito flakes**

Slice the cabbage thinly. A mandoline is ideal for this job. Remove the stems from the kale and slice into very fine ribbons. Grate the carrot and squeeze tightly to remove excess moisture. Place all the vegetables in a large bowl and massage for a couple of minutes with clean hands. This softens them and makes the volume of vegetables easier to handle.

Whisk together the eggs, spring onion, ginger, fish sauce and soy sauce.

Add the tapioca starch or white rice flour and whisk until well mixed. Add this to the shredded vegetables. At first it may seem like there's not enough binding liquid for the fritters but keep stirring and tossing together for a few minutes. The cabbage will soften and the mix will feel more balanced.

Heat a generous glug of oil over a medium heat. Fry ¾ cup of the mixture for 2-3 minutes on each side until nice and golden. You'll need to spread out the cabbage a little once it's in the pan and you can pull any stray tendrils of liquid back into the fritter if it runs.

Place in a warm oven while you cook the remaining batter.

Serve immediately with toppings as desired.

MOROCCAN LAMB LASAGNE WITH CAULIFLOWER BÉCHAMEL

SERVES 6
DAIRY FREE (IF CHEESE OMITTED OR NON DAIRY CHEESE USED) | NUT FREE

I've been making my lasagne with cauliflower béchamel for so long, my family wouldn't expect it any other way. It's such a fab way to get a little bit of vege in there and it's wonderfully creamy. This dish is an easy one to adapt to dairy free.

LAMB RAGU

Olive oil for sautéing

1 medium **onion**, diced

4 **garlic cloves**, finely diced

500g **lamb mince**

2 teaspoons **ground cumin**

1 teaspoon **ground coriander**

1 teaspoon **smoked paprika**

1 teaspoon **dried oregano leaves**

2 teaspoons finely diced **fresh rosemary leaves**

1 x 400g canned **crushed tomatoes**

2 cups **tomato purée** or **passata**

½ cup **water**

CAULIFLOWER BÉCHAMEL

1 small **onion**, diced

1 **garlic clove**, finely diced

1 small or ½ large **cauliflower**, cut into florets

2 cups **low-salt chicken stock**

¼ cup **cream** (could use coconut cream or oat milk to make dairy free)

TO ASSEMBLE

375g **instant lasagna sheets**

2 cups (or more!) **grated mozzarella cheese**

Sea salt and **cracked black pepper** to taste

Meat method

Heat a glug of olive oil in a sauté pan over a medium heat. Add the onion and cook until translucent and tender. Add the garlic and cook for a further minute. Add the lamb mince and brown, using a wooden spoon to break up any chunks. Add the spices and herbs. Stir around for a minute or so. Add the canned tomatoes, tomato purée or passata and water. Bring to a boil and then simmer gently for 20 minutes. Season to taste.

Cauliflower béchamel method

Heat a glug of olive oil in a sauté pan (one with a lid) over a medium heat. Add the onion and cook until translucent and tender. Add the garlic and cook for a further minute. Add the cauliflower florets and the stock. Place the lid on the pan and bring to a boil. Reduce to a simmer and cook for 15-20 minutes with the lid slightly ajar until very tender.

Add the cream and use a powerful blender or a stick blender to blitz until you produce a silky smooth sauce. It should be thick but still pourable. Add a good grind of cracked black pepper.

Assembly method

Preheat oven to 180°C.

Pour half a cup of water into the bottom of your dish.

Place a layer of pasta on top. Top with ⅓ of the lamb mince. Gently spoon ⅓ of the cauliflower sauce on top. Cover with another layer of pasta. Repeat this two more times.

Bake covered with foil for 20 minutes. Uncover, sprinkle with the mozzarella and bake for a further 20 minutes uncovered. Leave to stand for 15-20 minutes before cutting. This helps the layers settle so it will be easier to serve.

COOK'S NOTE:
To make the lasagne dairy free, replace the cream in the cauliflower sauce with your favourite plant-based milk. Use a dairy free cheese to top it or leave the cheese off altogether and add extra passata and fresh herbs to the top. You could even use breadcrumbs for a non-traditional topping.

BEEF & MUSHROOM STEW WITH CHEDDAR & PARSLEY DUMPLINGS

SERVES 4-6
NUT FREE

This recipe reminds me of my favourite meals when I was a kid. I'm a good half-Irish gal so naturally love this kind of cosy dish. Dumplings on top of a bubbling stew is impossible for me to resist.

Olive oil for sautéing and roasting

1 **onion**, finely diced

3 **garlic cloves**, finely diced

1.2kg **stewing beef** (I used chuck), cut into bite-sized pieces

3 tablespoons **flour**

¾ cup **red wine**

2 cups **beef stock**

2 tablespoons **tomato paste**

250g **Swiss brown** or small **Portobello mushrooms**, sliced

1 tablespoon **fresh rosemary leaves**, finely diced

DUMPLINGS

250g **white spelt flour** (can also use regular flour)

3 teaspoons **baking powder**

120g room temperature **butter**, cut into cubes

1 cup **grated cheddar cheese**

Large handful **parsley**, roughly chopped

Large handful **spinach leaves**, roughly chopped

½ teaspoon **sea salt**

Cracked black pepper and additional **sea salt** for seasoning

100ml **milk**

Additional **grated cheese** for topping

Stew method

Preheat oven to 130°C.

Heat a generous glug of oil in a cast iron casserole dish over a medium heat. Cook the onion for 8-10 minutes until tender and translucent. Add the garlic and cook for a further minute. Remove from the pan and set aside. Dust the meat with the flour.

Add a little more oil to the pan and brown the meat for a few minutes in batches (overcrowding the pan will stop the meat browning). Set aside. Pour the wine, beef stock and tomato paste into the pan. Bring it to a simmer. Return the meat, onions and garlic to the dish. Stir through the mushrooms and rosemary. Place the lid on and cook for 4 hours. Remove the lid and cook for a further 30-40 minutes to thicken up the liquid. Remove from the oven. Season to taste.

Dumpling method

Heat the oven to 180°C.

Sift the flour and baking powder into a large bowl and mix together. Rub the butter into the flour until it resembles coarse breadcrumbs. Stir through the cheese, parsley and spinach. Add salt and cracked black pepper.

Make a large well in the flour and pour in the milk. Use a wooden spoon to incorporate the milk slowly into the flour. Try not to overmix.

Turn onto a lightly floured surface and knead for just a few moments to bring it together. Form into a long sausage shape and cut into 10 even pieces. Form each of these into a ball.

Make sure the stew is very hot. Arrange the dumplings on top. Cover with a lid or tin foil and bake for 30 minutes. Remove the lid, sprinkle the dumplings with the additional grated cheese and bake for a further 15 minutes until golden.

COOK'S TIP

The stew can be made a day or two in advance and will taste even better for it. Just make sure you heat the stew up until piping hot before adding the dumplings.

MEXICAN SPICED BEEF CHEEKS WITH CORIANDER & JALAPENO SAUCE

SERVES 4
GLUTEN FREE

The meat will benefit from being made the day before, if possible.

BEEF CHEEKS

Olive oil for sautéing
2 medium **brown onions**, sliced into rings
4 **garlic cloves**, finely diced
2 **red chillies**, seeds removed and finely diced
1 large **carrot**, peeled and coarsely grated
1 heaped teaspoon **ground cumin**
1 teaspoon **ground coriander**
½ teaspoon **ground cinnamon**
1 teaspoon **ground oregano**
2 large **beef cheeks** (about 800g total)
Sea salt and **cracked black pepper**
3 tablespoons **tomato paste**
1 tablespoon **balsamic vinegar**
2 cups **beef stock**

CORIANDER & JALAPENO SAUCE

1 small handful **fresh parsley**
2 handfuls **fresh coriander**
6 slices **pickled jalapeno** (more if desired)
Juice of 1 **lime** (or about 2 tablespoons)
⅓–½ cup **olive oil**
Generous pinch **salt**

GRAIN-FREE FLATBREADS
MAKES ROUGHLY 8 PIECES

1½ cups **tapioca flour**
1½ cups **almond meal**
1 cup **milk** (any kind will work)
¼ cup **olive oil**
½ teaspoon **salt**
½ teaspoon **gluten free baking powder**
1 free range **egg**

Beef cheeks

Preheat the oven to 140°C.

Heat a generous glug of olive oil over a medium heat. Add the onion and cook for 10 minutes until tender. Add the garlic, chilli and carrot. Sauté for another few minutes. Add the cumin, coriander, cinnamon and oregano. Toss well and cook for a minute. Spoon into the oven proof dish that you'll be using.

Wipe out the pan and add another glug of olive oil. Raise the heat slightly. Season the beef cheeks well and brown on both sides in the pan. Add to the oven dish.

Place the tomato paste, balsamic and stock in a small saucepan and bring to a boil. Pour over the beef cheeks. Place the lid on the dish or cover tightly with tin foil.

Place in the oven and cook for 4 hours. Remove the lid, turn the beef cheeks over and cook without a lid for 30 minutes more. Pour the liquid into a saucepan and simmer for about 20 minutes until it has reduced by half. Add back into the dish with the beef cheeks.

Pull meat apart into big chunks.

Can be stored in the fridge for up to 4 days.

Coriander & Jalapeno Sauce

Place all ingredients into a small jug and use a hand blender to blitz until relatively smooth. Taste and adjust seasoning as needed.

Will last up to 5 days in a jar in the fridge.

Grain-free flatbreads

Place all ingredients in a large bowl and whisk until smooth.

Heat a cast iron skillet or non-stick pan over a medium heat. Brush very lightly with oil.

Pour ¼ cup of batter into the pan and quickly swirl around as you would for a crêpe. Cook for a couple of minutes on each side until golden.

Leftover flatbreads can be gently heated in a dry skillet or wrapped in tin foil and heated in a medium-low oven.

CREAMY CHICKEN, CHICKPEA & SPINACH CURRY

SERVES 6
DAIRY FREE | GLUTEN FREE | NUT FREE

This recipe is an update of one of the most popular recipes from my last cookbook and my social media accounts. It's a lovely way to pack a ton of spinach into a tasty creamy sauce. It's a mild (but flavourful) curry that is good for the whole family.

The spinach will retain that gorgeous green unless it's cooked for a long time, so I add it at the end of the sauce creation and don't simmer it for too long with the chicken. It can lose some of its colour in subsequent reheatings but will still taste brilliant. These days I add chickpeas to this meal too. They are such an economical way to add a bit of bulk to the meal and I love their texture.

Oil for sautéing
1 **onion**, diced
1 tablespoon finely grated **ginger**
4 **garlic cloves**, finely diced
1 tablespoon **ground cumin**
1 teaspoon **garam masala**
½ teaspoon **ground turmeric**
¼ teaspoon **cayenne pepper** (optional)
1 x 400g canned **chopped tomatoes**
1 x 400g canned **coconut milk**
¾ cup **water**
½ teaspoon **salt**
500g **frozen spinach leaves**, thawed and squeezed of excess liquid
Juice of 1 **lemon**
800g free range **boneless chicken thighs**, cut into bite-sized chunks
1 x 400g canned **chickpeas**, drained and rinsed
Salt and **cracked black pepper** for seasoning

Heat a generous glug of oil in a large saucepan over a medium heat. Add the onion and cook for about 10 minutes until translucent and tender. Add the ginger and garlic. Sauté for a few minutes before adding all the spices. Add a little more oil if the pan is dry. Allow the spices 1-2 minutes in the pan to become fragrant before adding the tomatoes, coconut milk, water and salt. Bring to a boil before simmering for 10 minutes. Remove from the heat. Add the spinach and the lemon juice. Stir well.

Allow to cool slightly before using a blender, food processor or stick blender to blitz the sauce until smooth. Taste and adjust seasoning as needed. Sometimes a little more lemon juice is good.

Heat a glug of oil in a sauté pan over a high heat. Add the chicken and cook for 7 minutes, tossing regularly until browned. Add the chickpeas and the spinach sauce. Bring to a boil and then simmer for 5 minutes.

Serve with steamed rice, cauliflower rice or quinoa. Leftover curry will last 4 days in an airtight container in the fridge.

COOK'S TIP
This dish can be made with tofu or fish instead of chicken. The sauce could also be made in advance and split into smaller portions if needed and then frozen. Simply reheat and pair with the protein of your choosing to make a quick meal.

RICH MUSHROOM & FRENCH LENTIL PIE WITH CRUNCHY FILO TOPPING

SERVES 6
VEGETARIAN (IF VEGETABLE STOCK USED)

Mushrooms and lentils are such a delicious combination. It's one I turn to again and again.

The lentils can be cooked the day before (in fact I'd encourage it) and then all you need to do when it's time to eat is throw the buttered, scrunched filo pastry on top and bake for half an hour. If you do make the pie filling in advance, be sure to heat it up before placing the pastry on top. Cook the lentils in vegetable stock if you're vegetarian, otherwise use beef stock because the savoury richness it adds is wonderful.

700g small **Portobello** or **Swiss brown mushrooms**
Olive oil for sautéing
2 **onions**, finely diced
1 medium **carrot**, diced
4 **garlic cloves**, finely diced
1 tablespoon **fresh rosemary leaves**, finely diced
1 cup **French green lentils**, rinsed well
1 litre **beef stock** or **vegetable stock**
1 tablespoon **tomato paste**
Handful **fresh parsley**, roughly chopped
1 tablespoon **balsamic vinegar**
2 teaspoons **cornflour**
½ cup **fresh cream** (optional - reduce the stock by this amount if using)
8-10 sheets **filo pastry**
Melted **butter** for brushing
Sea salt and **cracked black pepper**

Dice half the mushrooms and cut the other half into quarters.

Heat a generous glug of oil in a large sauté pan. Add the onion and carrot. Cook for around 10 minutes until the onion is tender and translucent. Add the garlic, rosemary and the diced portion of the mushrooms. Cook for a few minutes until the mushrooms are glossy.

Add the lentils, stock, tomato paste and parsley. Bring to a boil and then simmer for 15 minutes. Add the rest of the mushrooms and the balsamic vinegar. Cook for a further 10 minutes.

Mix the cornflour with a few tablespoons of water and add to the lentils, stirring very quickly to ensure there are no lumps. Give this a few minutes on the heat to thicken up the liquid a little before setting aside.

Add the cream now if using. Taste and season well with sea salt and cracked black pepper. At this stage the lentils should have plenty of gravy to ensure the dish doesn't dry out when you bake it.

Preheat the oven to 180°C.

Spoon the lentil and mushroom filling into an oven proof dish (or several smaller dishes if you prefer). Brush each filo sheet with melted butter on both sides. Scrunch up each sheet and place on top of the filling. Repeat until you've covered most of the surface of the dish.

Bake for around 30 minutes or until the pastry is golden brown and the filling is bubbling.

GREEN RISOTTO

SERVES 4
GLUTEN FREE | NUT FREE | VEGETARIAN

A zingy, bright bowl of comfort. The pea purée that is stirred through at the end, and herbs used in the recipe, make for a simple but quite wonderful dish.

Olive oil for sautéing
1 medium **onion**, diced
4 **cloves garlic**, finely diced
1 teaspoon **dried tarragon**
1½ cups **Arborio rice**
¾ cup **white wine**
Zest of 1 **lemon**
5 cups **vegetable stock**
100g finely grated **Parmesan cheese**
Handful **fresh mint**, roughly chopped

PEA AND PARSLEY PURÉE

1 cup **frozen peas**, left to defrost for 30 minutes, then drained well
Large handful **fresh parsley**, roughly chopped
¼ cup **olive oil**

To serve: **fresh herbs**, drizzle of **extra virgin olive oil**

Place all the pea purée ingredients into a food processor and blitz until it has the texture of a rough pesto. Alternatively use a stick blender. Set aside until ready to use.

Heat the oil in a large sauté pan over a medium-low heat. Cook the onion and garlic gently, without browning, until translucent and tender. Add the tarragon and the rice. Ensure the rice is evenly coated in the oil. Cook for a minute, tossing constantly. Add the wine and the lemon zest and stir. Cook until the wine has been completely absorbed by the rice.

Bring the stock to a boil in a separate pot. Add the hot stock a half-cup at a time to the rice, allowing a few minutes between each addition for it to absorb. Keep the rice over a medium heat during this time and stir often. Keep doing this until you've used all the stock. Your risotto should be creamy but not gluggy or mushy. A little soupy is good as it will keep absorbing liquid as it cools. Add the pea purée. Heat through. Remove from the heat. Stir through the Parmesan and fresh mint. Season to taste.

Serve immediately with a little Parmesan sprinkled on top and a scattering of additional fresh herbs (if desired). I also like to drizzle with a little good quality olive oil.

ROAST CHICKEN & SOURDOUGH

SERVES 4
NUT FREE

This is, hands-down, my two daughters' favourite meal. They request it constantly and are so excited when it's on the menu. The chunks of sourdough are cooked with the chicken, absorbing all that amazing, rich flavour. The roasted bread is packed with the pan juices in some bites and crunchy in others. The key is to pre-soak the bread in chicken stock, olive oil and herbs so it doesn't dry out while roasting. It's a simple dish but so delicious. As I photographed this recipe for the book, my girls stood on either side of me choosing which pieces they wanted to eat as soon as I was done. I realise it looks all a bit brown in the picture but we always have this with a big salad or plenty of green vegetables.

1 medium or large free range **chicken**
½ cup **olive oil**, plus additional for drizzling
Sea salt and **cracked black pepper**
3-4 thick slices **stale sourdough**, cut into chunks
¾ cup **chicken stock**
3-4 stems **fresh rosemary**
6 **garlic cloves**
2 medium **onions**, peeled and quartered

Preheat the oven to 180℃.

Place the chicken in a large oven proof dish. Drizzle with olive oil and season well.

Place the bread chunks in a bowl. Toss with the stock and rosemary. Let the bread soak up all the liquid. Pour over the olive oil and season with sea salt and cracked black pepper. Place the bread all around the chicken along with the garlic and pieces of onion.

Roast for 1 ½ hours or until the chicken is cooked through. About halfway through the cooking, tilt the roasting dish so that all the juices from inside the chicken run into the rest of the dish. Turn the pieces of bread over a couple of times while cooking to let the soggy bits get crispy and the crispy bits become juicy. If you want to crisp the bread chunks up even more, remove the chicken from the pan when it's ready and place it on a plate to rest. Pop the bread back in the oven, raise the temperature to 200℃ and cook for a further 10 or so minutes.

SPICED SLOW ROASTED LAMB LEG WITH FRESH HERB SAUCE & POMEGRANATE SEEDS

SERVES 6
GLUTEN FREE | NUT FREE

I love a New Zealand lamb leg as an option for feeding a crowd. It can often be bought on special, and yields a large amount of meat. This is the way I've made it for years. Slow roasting means there's no carving, just gorgeously tender meat that pulls away easily from the bone.

Leftover lamb can go into pasta dishes or be added to soups, like my Everything Soup (pg 50).

2 tablespoons **brown sugar**
2 teaspoons **ground cumin**
1 teaspoon **garam masala**
Zest of 1 **lemon**
3 **garlic cloves**, finely diced
3 tablespoons **olive oil**
1 **onion**, cut into thick rings
1 **bone-in lamb leg**
1 cup **beef stock**

HERB SAUCE

Large handful **fresh mint**
Large handful **fresh parsley**
1 small **garlic clove**, finely diced
½ cup **olive oil**
Juice of 1 **lemon**
Sea salt and **cracked black pepper**

To garnish: **pomegranate seeds** (optional)

Preheat the oven to 200°C.

Combine the sugar, cumin, garam masala, lemon zest, garlic and olive oil in a bowl and stir well. Rub all over the lamb leg.

Lay the onion slices in the bottom of your roasting dish. Place the lamb leg on top. Cook for 25 minutes uncovered. Reduce the temperature to 150°C, pour the beef stock around the lamb (not on top) and cover tightly with foil. Cook for 3 hours. Remove the foil and cook for a final 30 minutes uncovered.

Pour off the liquid from the bottom of the pan into a saucepan. Simmer for 15 minutes until reduced by half. Cover the lamb with foil while you prepare the jus.

Blend together all the herb sauce ingredients until smooth. Season generously. To serve, place the lamb on a platter and pour over the jus. Garnish with pomegranate seeds and some of the herb sauce. Serve the rest of the herb sauce on the side.

VEGAN TRAY BAKE NACHOS WITH TOFU, MUSHROOM & LENTIL CHILLI

SERVES 4-6
GLUTEN FREE | VEGAN

This recipe is my absolute favourite meat-free chilli. A little different from many other recipes as it contains no beans at all. It's really well balanced in flavour and texture. Grated tofu is such a great way to add some good protein in there.

These nachos are a really delicious way to use the chilli, but you could also use it in tacos, in burritos or over rice.

Olive oil for sautéing
1 medium **brown onion**, diced
1 stalk **celery**, diced
1 large **carrot**, diced
4 **garlic cloves**, finely diced
2 teaspoons **ground cumin**
1 teaspoon **ground coriander**
1 teaspoon **smoked paprika**
200g **Portobello** or **Swiss brown mushrooms**, diced
300g block **firm tofu**, grated
1 x 390g canned **lentils**, drained and rinsed
1 x 400g can **chopped tomatoes**
1 tablespoon **tomato paste**
1 tablespoon **tamari** or **soy sauce**
Generous pinch **dried red chilli flakes**
Sea salt and **cracked black pepper**
180g (roughly) **corn chips**
1 cup (or more) **dairy free cheese**, grated
¼ **red onion**, finely diced
10 **cherry tomatoes**, quartered

To garnish: sliced **jalapenos**, thinly sliced **radish**, **guacamole** and **fresh coriander** to top

Heat a generous glug of oil in a sauté pan over a medium heat. Add the onion, celery and carrot. Cook, stirring frequently, for 10-15 minutes until the onion is tender and translucent. Add the garlic and cook for a further few minutes.

Add the cumin, ground coriander, paprika and diced mushrooms plus a generous pinch of salt. Sauté, stirring frequently, until the mushrooms are glossy and have released their liquid.

Add the grated tofu and lentils. Toss with the spices and vegetables for a minute or so before adding the canned tomatoes, tomato paste, tamari and chilli flakes. Fill the tomato can half-full with water and add this also. Bring to the boil and simmer for 10 minutes. Taste and season as desired with sea salt and cracked black pepper.

Chilli can be stored in an airtight container in the fridge for up to 5 days.

To assemble nachos

Scatter corn chips over a medium-sized oven proof tray. Top with big dollops of the tofu chilli. You may not need all that you've made but be sure to be generous. Top with the grated dairy free cheddar. Grill until bubbling hot. Top with the diced red onion, cherry tomatoes, jalapenos, radish and dollops of guacamole. Finish with a scattering of roughly chopped coriander. Serve immediately.

BROCCOLI & GREENS TART WITH BUCKWHEAT & BROWN RICE CRUST

SERVES 4-6
GLUTEN FREE | NUT FREE | VEGETARIAN

This gluten free pastry is forgiving and will come together easily for you.

TART

½ cup **tapioca flour**
½ cup **buckwheat flour**
1 cup **brown rice flour**
½ teaspoon **sea salt**
75g cold **butter**, cut into cubes
1 free range **egg**
1-2 tablespoons **cold water**, as needed

FILLING

olive oil for sautéing
1 medium **onion**, diced
1 **garlic clove**, finely diced
½ medium head **broccoli**
2 large **leaves silverbeet** or **chard**, roughly chopped
4 free range **eggs**, lightly whisked
½ cup **cream**
¾ cup grated **cheese**
½ teaspoon **dried tarragon**
Sea salt and **cracked black pepper**

Pastry Method

Place the flours and salt into a food processor along with the butter. Pulse until the butter is completely incorporated. Add the egg and pulse until evenly mixed through. Add 1 tablespoon of water, allowing 5 seconds of mixing before deciding whether to add more. You can press the pastry dough between your fingers to see if it has come together with the consistency of play dough. You may only need 1 tablespoon. Add another if needed. Bring the dough together into a ball, wrap it in cling film or baking paper and place in the fridge for 20 minutes.

Preheat oven to 180°C. Remove pastry from the fridge and roll out on a floured piece of baking paper until slightly less than 1cm thick. Use the paper to help you drape it over a loose-bottomed rectangular tart dish and gently press into the groves. Use a knife to trim the top edge. Patch up any tears in the pastry and prick the bottom a few times with a fork. Place in the fridge or freezer to chill for 10 minutes. Bake for 12-15 minutes until firm and very slightly golden. Set aside to cool completely.

Filling Method

Increase oven to 200°C.

Heat a generous glug of oil in a sauté pan over a medium heat. Add the onion and cook until tender and translucent. Add the garlic and cook for another couple of minutes. Use a box grater to grate the broccoli. Add this to the pan, raise the heat to high and cook for 2 minutes before stirring through the silverbeet and removing from the heat.

Whisk together the egg, cream, cheese and tarragon. Season well. Mix through the vegetables.

Spoon this into the crust. Place in the oven and bake for roughly 30 minutes until the filling is lightly firm and golden.

COOK'S TIP:
If you're not a fan of the flavour of buckwheat flour, you can replace it with a ¾ cup almond meal.

130
Quinoa, Spring Onion
& Parmesan Patties

132
Easy Flaxseed
Crackers

134
Spelt Scones
with Two Cheeses
& Spinach

136
Walnut, Oat &
Parmesan Savoury
Biscuits

138
Panko-Crumbed
Tofu Fingers with
Spicy Mayo

140
Creamy Garlic
Mushrooms

142
Fancy Kiwi
Onion Dip

144
Broccoli & Cheese
Fritters with Garlic
& Mint Yoghurt

146
The Best Egg Salad

148
Potted Smoked
Fish with Lemon,
Horseradish & Dill

150
Very Crunchy Roast
Potatoes

152
Sautéed Red Cabbage
with Apple Cider
Vinegar

154
Beetroot Cured
Salmon with Lemon &
Caper Cream

156
Sourdough Stuffing
with Bacon, Celery &
Apple

Sides & Snacky Things

QUINOA, SPRING ONION & PARMESAN PATTIES

MAKES 10-15 PATTIES
GLUTEN FREE (IF GF FLOUR IS USED) | NUT FREE | VEGETARIAN

Cumin and turmeric in the same patty as Parmesan cheese might sound a little unusual but it really really works. Serve these with mayonnaise you've spiked with smoked paprika, lime and a little chilli.

Wonderful with drinks or as a light meal alongside a big green salad.

1 cup **quinoa**
2 cups **vegetable** or **chicken stock**
2 large **garlic cloves**, finely diced
1 teaspoon **ground cumin**
½ teaspoon **ground turmeric**
1 cup finely grated **Parmesan cheese**
2 **spring onions**, green parts, finely sliced
Handful **fresh parsley**, roughly chopped
1 free range **egg**
2 tablespoons **flour** (any will work)
Cracked black pepper
Olive oil for sautéing

Rinse the quinoa well. Place in a medium saucepan with the stock and bring to a boil. Reduce heat to a simmer and cook with a lid very slightly ajar for around 15 minutes until tender and the liquid has been absorbed. Put the lid on and leave to sit for 5 minutes.

Stir through the garlic, cumin, turmeric, Parmesan, spring onion and parsley. Leave to cool for 15 minutes before mixing in the egg, flour and a generous seasoning of ground black pepper.

Form heaped spoonfuls of mixture into patties. Place in the fridge for at least 30 minutes to firm up.

Heat a generous glug of oil in a sauté pan over a medium heat. Cook the patties until golden brown on both sides. Keep warm in the oven until ready to serve.

EASY FLAXSEED CRACKERS

GLUTEN FREE | NUT FREE | VEGAN

These crackers bring the crunch! They're super quick and easy. Spread out on a tray and then snap into pieces when done. Top with all your favourite things.

¾ cup **flaxseeds**
¼ cup each: **sesame seeds, sunflower seeds, pumpkin seeds**
1 tablespoon **ground psyllium husk**
½ teaspoon **garlic powder**
1 teaspoon **dried thyme**
½ teaspoon **fine salt**
1 tablespoon **olive oil**
1¼ cups **boiling water**

To garnish: **flaky sea salt**

Preheat oven to 160℃.

Place all the dry ingredients in a large bowl and mix. Add the olive oil and water and mix very well. Leave to sit for 5 minutes.

Pour the mixture onto a large (lined) oven tray and spread out thinly using a spatula or the back of a spoon. Keeping the spoon or spatula damp makes this much easier. If you don't have a very large oven tray, split the mixture in half and use two trays.

Bake for 40 minutes, turning over the sheet of crackers after 30 mins. Sprinkle with flaky sea salt while still warm. Allow to cool completely before breaking into pieces and storing in an airtight container for up to 10 days.

SPELT SCONES WITH TWO CHEESES & SPINACH

SERVES 6-8
NUT FREE | VEGETARIAN

When our eldest daughter was a toddler we had a family summertime coffee business in a converted shipping container in Northland, New Zealand. We were known for my mother-in-law's incredibly good cheese scones. This is my version of her wonderful recipe.

- 2½ cups **white spelt flour** (regular flour will work too)
- 3 teaspoons **baking powder**
- 100g **butter**, at room temperature, cut into cubes
- 1 teaspoon **fine sea salt**
- Generous grind **cracked black pepper**
- 1 cup **strong cheddar cheese**, grated (plus additional for topping)
- ½ cup finely grated **Parmesan cheese**
- 2 big handfuls **baby spinach**, roughly chopped
- 1 cup **milk**

Preheat the oven to 220°C.

Sift the flour and baking powder into a large bowl. Rub the butter into the flour until it resembles coarse breadcrumbs. Stir through the salt and pepper. (Lots of cracked pepper is lovely in these). Add the cheeses and chopped spinach. Stir well.

Create a well and pour the milk into the middle. Use a wide knife or a spatula to very quickly bring the mixture together. Do not over mix.

Turn onto a well floured board. Press the dough into a soft rectangle shape. Cut into 12 roughly even pieces. This is a sticky dough. You'll find coating your knife (and also your hands) in flour can make handling the scones easier.

Place on a baking sheet lined with paper. Leave some space between each scone but let them be close enough that they will expand and end up touching each other a little. This creates a lovely tear apart look to your batch. Sprinkle cheese on the top of each scone.

Bake for approx 15 minutes or until golden brown.

WALNUT, OAT & PARMESAN SAVOURY BISCUITS

MAKES ROUGHLY 24 BISCUITS
VEGETARIAN

Serve these with delicious spreads (especially herby ones), cured meats, soft cheeses, or just nibble on their own. I quite like crumbling them over a bowl of vegetable soup. Just delightful.

1 cup **rolled oats**
¾ cup **raw walnuts**
1 cup **white spelt flour** or **regular flour**
½ teaspoon **salt**
75g **butter**
1 free range **egg**
1 teaspoon finely diced **fresh rosemary** or ½ teaspoon **dried rosemary**
¾ cup finely grated **Parmesan cheese**
Good pinch **cayenne pepper**

Preheat the oven to 170°C.

Place the oats and walnuts in a food processor. Blitz to a coarse crumb.

Add the flour and salt. Mix well. Add the remaining ingredients and process for a few minutes, scraping down the sides every now and then until the dough is well combined.

Place in the fridge for 10 minutes to cool and allow the dough to bind together.

Line an oven proof tray with baking paper. Roll teaspoons of dough into balls and place on the tray evenly spaced. You'll be able to fit around 12 at a time.

Use the bottom of a heavy glass with a wide base to flatten each ball into a round biscuit with a lovely rustic edge. Use a small piece of baking paper between the cracker and the glass to ensure it doesn't stick.

Bake for 12-15 minutes until lightly browned.

Gently slide the sheet of baking paper off the tray to continue to cool. You can then lift them onto another sheet of baking paper with crackers that you've prepared while the first batch was cooking.

If it's a very hot day it can be helpful to put any crackers that are waiting to be baked into the freezer to keep cool. This will ensure the butter doesn't melt too fast while baking and gives an even cooking result.

Cooled biscuits can be stored in an airtight container in a cool pantry for up to 10 days.

PANKO-CRUMBED TOFU FINGERS WITH SPICY MAYO

SERVES 4 AS A SNACK
NUT FREE | VEGETARIAN

Watch out if I'm around a plate of these because they'll all disappear! Crunchy and tasty, and great for even the tofu-sceptical.

300g **firm tofu**
¾ cup **flour**
1 teaspoon **smoked paprika**
1 teaspoon **Cajun spice mix**
1 teaspoon **salt**
2 free range **eggs**, lightly whisked
2 cups **panko breadcrumbs**
½ cup **One Minute Mayo** (pg 168) or good quality store bought **mayonnaise**
Hot sauce to taste
Olive oil for frying

To serve: **lemon wedges**

Cut the block of tofu into 1½ cm wide fingers. Lay out on a clean tea towel or some paper towels and blot really well.

Mix the flour with the smoked paprika, Cajun spice and salt. Place this in a shallow bowl suitable for using to coat the tofu. Place the egg and the breadcrumbs in their own, separate bowls.

Roll each piece of tofu in the seasoned flour, dip in the egg and then coat well with breadcrumbs. Repeat until all the pieces are crumbed.

Heat 1½ cm of oil in a sauté pan over a medium heat.

Cook the tofu fingers until golden on each side. Mix together the mayonnaise and as much hot sauce as desired to taste.

Serve immediately with the spicy mayo and some lemon wedges.

CREAMY GARLIC MUSHROOMS

SERVES 4 AS A SIDE
GLUTEN FREE | NUT FREE | VEGAN (IF DAIRY FREE OPTION USED)

Mushrooms are one of my absolute favourite foods. When I was pregnant with my eldest daughter, they were one of my most intense cravings. I just couldn't get enough.

It's pretty hard to resist mushrooms when cooked like this. Serve with poached eggs and sourdough, on top of steak, stirred through pasta or eaten straight from the pan as I did on the day I shot this recipe.

Here I've used a combination of Portobello, enoki and oyster mushrooms. Use whatever mushrooms are readily available and that you enjoy.

Olive oil for sautéing

400-450g **mushrooms**, sliced or broken into bite-sized pieces

Sea salt and **cracked black pepper**

3 **garlic cloves**, finely diced

2 teaspoons finely diced **fresh rosemary** or 1 teaspoon **dried rosemary**

1-2 tablespoons **balsamic vinegar**

½ cup **fresh cream** (or a mix of **oat milk** and **coconut cream** for dairy free)

Heat a generous glug of olive oil in a skillet over a high heat. Add the mushrooms and a generous pinch of salt. Toss regularly. The mushrooms will start to release liquid and become glossy. Stop stirring for a minute or so to allow the mushrooms to start to catch on the bottom of the pan and brown a little.

Reduce the heat to medium, push the mushrooms to the side, add a little more oil and cook the garlic and rosemary for a minute. Stir everything together again and add the balsamic vinegar.

Cook for a further minute before adding the cream. Let the cream heat through and bubble a little before removing from the heat and adding a good seasoning of cracked black pepper.

Taste and add more salt if needed.

FANCY KIWI ONION DIP

SERVES 4-6 AS A SNACK
GLUTEN FREE | NUT FREE

I find a chip and dip situation quite hard to resist. This homemade version of our iconic New Zealand dip is easy to make and tastes fantastic. Onions are sautéed low and slow until they are tender and lightly caramelised. I love this on a platter with my favourite potato chips and a bunch of raw veges for variety and colour.

Olive oil for sautéing
3 medium **onions**, thinly sliced
Salt and **cracked black pepper**
1 small **garlic clove**, finely diced
1 tablespoon **Worcestershire sauce**
1 teaspoon **balsamic vinegar**
250g **crème fraîche**
Juice of 1 **lemon** (as needed)

To garnish: finely chopped **chives** or **spring onion** (optional)

Heat a generous glug of olive oil in a sauté pan over a low-medium heat. Add the onion along with a good pinch of salt and cook gently for 20 minutes or more, stirring regularly until the onion is very tender and lightly browned. Lower the heat if they are cooking too quickly. Add the garlic and sauté for a few minutes. Add the Worcestershire sauce and vinegar and cook for one last minute.

Remove from the pan and place in the fridge to cool completely.

Roughly chop the cooked onion. Mix through the crème fraîche along with a good squeeze of lemon. Season well with salt and cracked pepper.

Garnish with chopped chives or spring onion before serving.

BROCCOLI & CHEESE FRITTERS WITH GARLIC & MINT YOGHURT

MAKES 14–16 FRITTERS
GLUTEN FREE | NUT FREE | VEGETARIAN

I've always got time to enjoy a good fritter straight from the pan. Those fritters that do manage to make it to a serving plate are great with a simple garlic and mint yoghurt.

1 medium head **broccoli**, cut into florets
3 free range **eggs**
½ cup **milk**
1 large **garlic clove**, finely diced
1 teaspoon **ground cumin**
½ cup **tapioca flour** (if using **regular flour** or **all-purpose gluten free flour**, increase to ¾ cup to get the correct binding)
½ teaspoon **gluten free baking powder**
1½ cups grated **edam** or **cheddar cheese**
Sea salt and **cracked black pepper**
Olive oil for frying

GARLIC & MINT YOGHURT
1 cup **full fat Greek yoghurt**
1 large **garlic clove**, finely diced
Handful **fresh mint leaves**, roughly chopped
Zest of 1 **lime** or **lemon**

To serve: additional **fresh mint leaves, lime wedges**

Combine all the yoghurt sauce ingredients in a bowl and mix well. Season generously with salt and cracked black pepper. Store in the fridge until ready to use.

Steam broccoli florets until just tender. Set aside for 10 minutes to cool on a tea towel. This will get rid of excess liquid. Roughly dice.

Whisk together the eggs, milk, garlic, cumin, flour, baking powder and grated cheese. Season well. Stir through broccoli.

Heat a good glug of olive oil in a sauté pan over a medium heat. Cook heaped tablespoons of fritter mixture (you should be able to fit four at a time in the pan). Spread the broccoli pieces out a little over the surface of the fritter before flipping. You can also tidy up any stray tendrils of batter with a spatula or back of a spoon. Cook for 3 minutes on both sides until golden brown.

Repeat until all the batter is used.

Serve fritters with the yoghurt dip on the side.

THE BEST EGG SALAD

SERVES 2-3
GLUTEN FREE | NUT FEE | VEGETARIAN

Egg salad is my favourite easy lunch on a busy work day. When well made, there's really nothing better. As a filling in sandwiches, on crackers, straight from the bowl or my fav - on hot, buttery, very-thin grainy toast. Toasted pumpkin seeds on top for crunch.

6 free range **eggs**, hard boiled
⅓ cup **One Minute Mayo** (pg 168) or good quality store bought **mayonnaise**
Handful **fresh dill**, finely diced (or 1 teaspoon dried dill tips)
1½ tablespoons **capers**
2 tablespoons finely diced **red onion**
Sea salt and **cracked black pepper**

Mash the eggs and the mayonnaise together well, before stirring through the other ingredients. Taste and season generously.

POTTED SMOKED FISH WITH LEMON, HORSERADISH & DILL

SERVES 4-6 AS A SNACK
GLUTEN FREE | NUT FREE

This traditional method of preserving smoked fish is especially delicious with toasted or freshly baked sourdough. I'll happily eat it on toast for lunch, or maybe alongside a bowl of vegetable soup - yum!

Lots of different types of smoked fish will work well in this recipe. Get some advice from your fishmonger if you're not sure which variety will best suit your tastes.

225g **butter**
300g **smoked fish**, skin and bones removed
Zest and **juice** of 1 **lemon**
1 tablespoon **horseradish sauce**
Small handful **fresh dill**, finely chopped
1 tablespoon **fresh thyme leaves**
Pinch **cayenne pepper** (more if you enjoy the heat)
Cracked black pepper

The first step is to clarify the butter (remove the milk solids). Cut the butter into a few smaller pieces and place in a small saucepan over a low heat. Let it bubble very very gently, without stirring at all, until the milk solids have separated from the butterfat and start to sink to the bottom. You'll be able to push the foam on top to the side slightly and see the very pure golden liquid. This will take about 15 minutes. Skim the foam from the top and pour through a fine strainer or muslin. Set aside.

You'll need the clarified butter to be liquid for this recipe so don't place it in the fridge or make it too far in advance of your fish preparation.

Break the smoked fish into small chunks. Place into a bowl along with the lemon zest and juice, the horseradish sauce, dill, thyme and cayenne pepper. Add a good grind of cracked black pepper. Mix well. Pour over ¾ of your clarified butter and stir to combine thoroughly. Taste and adjust seasoning if you like. Add more lemon juice or horseradish to suit your own taste. You shouldn't need any salt.

Press the fish mixture really firmly into a medium sized jar or a few smaller ramekins. Use a fork to press down and make sure the fish is packed in as tightly as possible. Pour some of the remaining butter over the top to seal it. I like to seal a few additional bits of the herbs in the butter on top. Place in the fridge to set for at least an hour.

Bring to almost room temperature before serving.

The fish will last a week in the fridge while still sealed by the solid clarified butter on top. Eat within three days once unsealed.

VERY CRUNCHY ROAST POTATOES

SERVES 4 AS A SIDE
GLUTEN FREE | NUT FREE | VEGAN

Truly crunchy roast potatoes are the best. Here in Aotearoa it has to be Agria potatoes for the best result. This might be controversial but I've never been able to get the same amazing crunch with any other variety.

700g **Agria potatoes**, washed and cut into 4-5cm chunks
Olive oil for roasting
Sea salt and **cracked black pepper**

Preheat the oven to 230°C.

Place potatoes in a large pot of water. Bring to a boil and cook for 10 minutes before tipping into a colander to drain. Leave in the colander to dry out for 5 minutes.

Drizzle the potatoes VERY generously with olive oil and sprinkle generously with sea salt and cracked black pepper. Toss well.

Place on a lined large baking tray (you want the potatoes to have plenty of space to crisp up).

Roast for 25-35 minutes until really crunchy. Flip just once during the cooking process.

SAUTÉED RED CABBAGE WITH APPLE CIDER VINEGAR

SERVES 4 AS A SIDE DISH
GLUTEN FREE | NUT FREE | VEGAN

Don't doubt this simple side dish. It's such a hearty, vibrant, wintery joy.

The trick is to add the cabbage to a very hot skillet and not be in a hurry to toss it so you can get some nicely browned and crisped-up bits first. The splash of apple cider vinegar at the end adds a bright flavour and also brings back the rich pinky purple colour that can disappear in the cooking process.

Use a mandoline to slice the cabbage if you can. It makes prepping cabbage so fast and you get nice even slices. It's a kitchen tool you can pick up relatively inexpensively. I've had the same cheapish one for at least 10 years.

¼ cup **olive oil** for sautéing
½ medium **red cabbage**, sliced thinly
Sea salt
1 tablespoon **apple cider vinegar**

Place a dry skillet (ideally cast iron) over a high heat. Once hot add the olive oil and follow immediately with the cabbage. Leave for 1 minute before starting to move the cabbage around the pan. Add a generous sprinkle of sea salt and keep tossing the cabbage regularly.

Sauté for 5 minutes until the cabbage has become tender. Add the apple cider vinegar to the pan and cook for a further minute or so. Taste and season more if needed before serving.

BEETROOT CURED SALMON WITH LEMON & CAPER CREAM

SERVES 10 AS A SNACK
GLUTEN FREE | NUT FREE

Cured salmon has such a delicious, delicate but rich flavour. I think of it as particularly great for entertaining at times such as Christmas, but you'd absolutely enjoy this any time of the year. Beetroot cured salmon is visually striking but also quite simple to make. Ensure you've got a very sharp knife for slicing the salmon once it's cured. It's essential to be able to get beautifully thin slices.

1½ medium **beetroot**, grated
2 tablespoons **salt**
2 tablespoons **caster sugar**
60mls **vodka** or **gin**
⅓ cup finely chopped **fresh dill**
Zest of 1 **lemon**
1 side of **salmon** (around 1kg)

LEMON & CAPER CREAM
150g **crème fraîche** or **sour cream**
Zest of 1 **lemon**
2 tablespoons **capers**
Sea salt and **cracked black pepper**

To serve: **toasted sourdough** or **baguette** slices, **cucumber** slices, **caperberries** (optional), and **fresh dill**

Combine the grated beetroot, salt, sugar, gin, dill and lemon zest in a bowl. Stir well.

Line a large dish with two layers of baking paper (leave plenty of paper to hang over the sides) and place the salmon on top skin side down. Smear evenly with the beetroot mixture. Wrap the baking paper around the salmon and cover with one or two layers of plastic film so that it is snugly wrapped. Place a slightly smaller dish or tray on top of the salmon and place a heavier item (like a small cast iron pan) on top to act as a weight. Leave the salmon for two days in the fridge. You can remove the weight after 24 hours. Drain off any excess liquid once a day.

Remove all the wrapping from the salmon and rinse it quickly under cold water. Pat dry thoroughly with paper towels and store in an airtight container.

Combine the crème fraîche, lemon and capers. Season well with salt and cracked black pepper.

Serve with salmon on top of slices of toasted bread with a generous spread of the caper and lemon cream, a cucumber slice, fresh dill and a caperberry if using. Finish with a good grind of cracked black pepper.

The salmon, once cured, will last a week in an airtight container in the fridge.

SOURDOUGH STUFFING WITH BACON, CELERY & APPLE

SERVES 4-6 AS A SIDE
NUT FREE

This is wonderful. Though it's called stuffing, it doesn't see the inside of a chook at all, and instead resembles a rich, savoury bread and butter pudding. It's a brilliant side dish alongside roasted meat.

½ loaf **sourdough bread** (about 270g), torn or cut into 4-5cm chunks

Olive oil for sautéing

1 medium **onion**, diced

1 stem **celery**, diced

3 **garlic cloves**, finely diced

120g streaky free range **bacon**, cut into 1cm pieces

3 tablespoons **butter**

1 **apple**, peeled and cut into 1cm pieces

1 tablespoon finely chopped **rosemary leaves**

1 tablespoon **fresh sage leaves**, finely chopped or 1 teaspoon **dried sage**

Cracked black pepper

1½ cups **chicken stock**

1 free range **egg**

Preheat the oven to 180°C.

Place the torn sourdough on an oven proof tray and toast for 5 minutes. Leave to cool.

Heat a generous glug of olive oil in a sauté pan over a medium heat. Add the onion, celery, garlic and bacon. Cook until the onion is tender and translucent. Add the butter, apple and herbs. Add some cracked black pepper. Cook for 2 minutes. Add the sourdough and toss well. Add half the stock and stir through so the bread is evenly coated.

Let the stuffing cool for 20 minutes before spooning into a well-greased oven proof dish. At this stage you could pop the stuffing in the fridge until you are ready to bake it (up to 24 hours beforehand).

Whisk together the remaining stock and the egg. Pour over the stuffing evenly. Cover with foil. Bake for 1 hour. Remove foil halfway through cooking.

162
Chicken Broth

164
Toasted Seeds

166
Seedy Yoghurt Flatbreads

168
One Minute Mayo

170
Chilli & Garlic Oil

172
The Dressing for Everything

174
Honey, Berry & Rosemary Shrub

176
Flavoured Butters

178
The Easiest One Bowl Gluten Free Pizza Base

180
Dukkah

182
Green Tea Infused Coconut Water

184
Non-alcoholic White Sangria

186
Turmeric, Cinnamon & Ginger Latte Paste

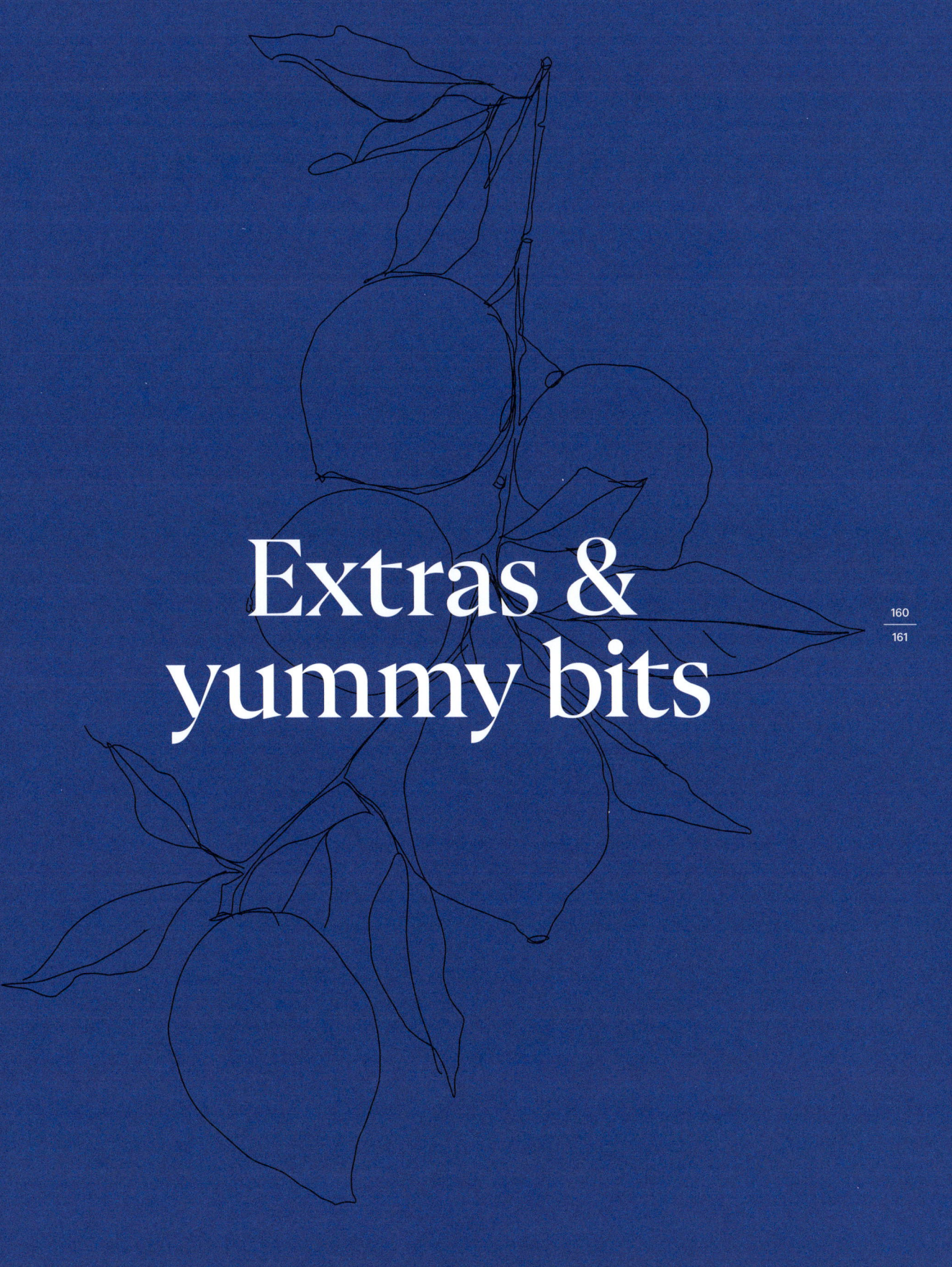

Extras & yummy bits

CHICKEN BROTH

GLUTEN FREE | NUT FREE

Chicken broth is made weekly in my kitchen for most of the year. We use it in soups and love sipping it from a mug in winter. A flavourful chicken broth is such a magnificent thing, full of nutrition and soul-satisfying flavour that is incredibly comforting on a cold day.

COOK'S TIP:
When I know I want to use my broth specifically for something like a clear Asian-inspired soup, I simmer the chicken bones with just 1 whole spring onion and a few cloves of garlic. This gives you a broth that has a lovely simple flavour that will allow you to build other flavours on top of it.

Another fantastic broth combination is a thumb-sized piece of both turmeric and ginger, peeled and cut into a few pieces with 1 whole spring onion, 10 black peppercorns and a head of garlic. Simmer as above. This is a fav for sipping during the cold and flu season.

BROTH USING A WHOLE RAW CHICKEN

I love that this method yields both a tasty broth and chicken meat that can be used in a variety of ways.

1 large free range **chicken**
2 **brown onions**, cut into quarters
1 head **garlic**, sliced across the very top to expose the cloves
2 medium **carrots**, cut into chunks
1 stalk **celery**
15 **whole black peppercorns**
Handful **parsley stalks** (optional)
1 tablespoon **dried dill tips** (optional)

Place the chicken and all the other ingredients except the dill and parsley in a large pot. Cover with 5-6 litres of water. Bring to a boil, removing any scum that comes to the surface. Reduce the temperature to a gentle simmer and cook for 1 hour. Very carefully lift the chicken from the water and remove all the meat. Place the skin and bones back in the water and simmer for 6-8 hours. Add the parsley and dill in the last 30 minutes of cooking. Strain the broth well, season very generously and store in the fridge for up to one week. Can be frozen for up to six months.

BROTH WITH LEFTOVER BONES FROM A ROAST CHICKEN

The flavour of broth made from using leftovers from a roast chicken is pretty darn wonderful.

1 leftover **roast chicken carcass**
2 **brown onions**, cut into quarters
1 head **garlic**, sliced across the very top to expose the cloves
2 medium **carrots**, cut into chunks
1 stalk **celery**
15 **whole black peppercorns**
Handful **parsley stalks** (optional)
1 tablespoon **dried dill tips** (optional)

Place the chicken bones and vegetables (except dill and parsley) in a large pot. Cover with 5-6 litres of water. Bring to a boil, removing any scum that comes to the surface. Reduce the temperature to a simmer and cook for 6-8 hours. Add the dill and parsley in the last 30 minutes of cooking. Strain well, season generously and store in the fridge for up to one week. Can be frozen for up to six months.

TOASTED SEEDS

MAKES 1¼ CUP OF EACH
GLUTEN FREE | NUT FREE (IF ONLY SEEDS USED) | VEGAN

Having delicious crunchy seeds like this on hand makes livening up a salad so easy. They're also great on top of eggs, soups and avocado on toast. Below is the seed combination that I usually use. I've shared 3 of my favourite ways to flavour them.

½ cup sunflower seeds
½ cup pumpkin seeds
¼ cup sesame seeds

Other additions that work well: Almonds, whole or roughly chopped, pistachios, cashew nuts, buckwheat, coconut flakes.

TAMARI, HONEY & CHILLI

4 teaspoons **tamari** or **soy sauce**
1 teaspoon **honey**
Generous pinch **dried red chilli flakes**

Toast the seeds in a dry skillet over a medium heat until lightly golden. Remove from the heat and drizzle tamari, honey and dried red chilli flakes. Toss the seeds with the seasoning quickly, letting the heat of the pan soften the honey and help the seeds absorb the flavour. Leave to cool completely before storing in an airtight jar.

SMOKY SAVOURY SEEDS

½ teaspoon **smoked paprika**
½ teaspoon **onion powder**
½ teaspoon **ground cumin**
2 teaspoons **tamari** or **soy sauce**
Squeeze of **lemon juice**

Toast the seeds in a dry skillet over a medium heat until lightly golden. Add smoked paprika, onion powder and ground cumin. Toss the seeds for one minute to allow the spices to become more fragrant. Remove from the heat and add the tamari and a little squeeze of lemon juice. Make sure everything is evenly coated. Leave to cool completely before storing in an airtight jar.

ROSEMARY, MAPLE & SEA SALT

1 teaspoon **pure maple syrup**
1 teaspoon finely diced **fresh rosemary leaves**
Flaky sea salt
Cracked black pepper

Toast the seeds in a dry skillet over a medium heat until lightly golden. Remove from the heat and drizzle with pure maple syrup and fresh rosemary leaves. Toss to evenly coat seeds and then add a generous pinch of flaky sea salt and a good grind of cracked black pepper. Stir through. Leave to cool completely before storing in an airtight jar.

SEEDY YOGHURT FLATBREADS

MAKES 6 PIECES
NUT FREE | VEGETARIAN

The addition of homemade bread makes even a simple bowl of soup feel a bit more special. This very easy recipe is as complicated as my breadmaking gets. Serve alongside your favourite salads, dip into extra virgin olive oil or load up with barbecued meat and tasty dips.

1½ cups **self raising flour**
½ cup **mixed seeds** (I used pumpkin, sunflower and sesame seeds)
1½ teaspoons **salt**
1½ teaspoon **baking powder**
250g **Greek yoghurt**

Mix together the flour, seeds, salt and baking powder. Add the yoghurt and use a wooden spoon to bring it all together. Knead for a minute, using well floured hands. The dough will be sticky and a bit shaggy. Place in a bowl and cover with a plate. Leave to sit for 30 minutes.

Cut the dough into six roughly even pieces.

Roll out on a lightly floured board until fairly thin.

Heat a dry pan (cast iron is ideal) on high. Cook the flatbreads for 1-2 minutes on each side until cooked through and browned.

ONE MINUTE MAYO

MAKES 1½ CUPS
GLUTEN FREE | NUT FREE | VEGETARIAN

Are you making your own mayonnaise yet? You have to! The process couldn't be easier. It's so much healthier to make it at home with good quality oil and is truly a gateway to lots of delicious eating.

Mayo can be turned into the best condiment ever with the addition of spices. Think turmeric or curry powder, or smoked paprika or sriracha. Oh, with finely chopped kimchi - so good! Enjoy with roast veges, in sandwiches and burgers or with crunchy dishes like my Panko Crumbed Tofu Fingers (pg 138).

Easy lunches such as chicken waldorf salad or delicious herby mashed eggs all start with great mayo.

You'll need a stick blender for my method.

1 free range **egg**
Generous pinch **salt**
1 teaspoon **apple cider vinegar**
1 cup **light olive oil**
2 teaspoons **lemon juice**
½ teaspoon **wholegrain mustard** (optional)

To season: **sea salt** and **cracked black pepper**

Use the jug that came with your stick blender for this. It's important to have a tight-ish fit for the blending head. Carefully crack the egg into the bottom of the jug. Sprinkle it with salt and add the vinegar. Pour over half the oil (preferably without breaking the yolk).

Place the stick blender over the yolk, turn on and hold to the bottom of the jug for 10-15 seconds. Once the egg and oil has started emulsifying, add the remaining oil in two lots, blending until thickened between each. It should come together and become very thick and creamy within 30 - 60 seconds. Stir through the lemon juice and mustard.

Taste and season as desired.

Store in an airtight jar in the fridge for up to a week.

CHILLI & GARLIC OIL

MAKES 1 CUP
GLUTEN FREE | NUT FREE | VEGAN

It's absurdly easy to make this at home and honestly, a bit magical. The process of heating oil with chilli and garlic creates a profound transformation to an incredibly versatile condiment.

Aside from the obvious uses for this (with dumplings, noodle soups, stir fries etc.), it's also amazing on scrambled and fried eggs, in cucumber salads with spring onions, over roasted tomatoes, tossed through pasta, on pizza and thousands of other ways you'll discover because you'll want to make it over and over again.

1 cup **light** or **extra light olive oil**
¼ cup **dried red chilli flakes**
3 **garlic cloves**, peeled and halved
½ teaspoon **salt**

Pour the oil, chilli flakes and garlic into a small pan. I use a 16cm cast-iron skillet.

Place over a low-medium heat. You are aiming to have tiny bubbles around the rim of the skillet breaking the surface, but nothing more intense than that. The olive oil shouldn't bubble vigorously or smoke. Leave to heat gently for 5 minutes. Turn off the heat and stir through the salt. Leave to cool completely before removing the garlic.

Store in an airtight container in a cool, dark place. Will last a month or more.

THE DRESSING FOR EVERYTHING

GLUTEN FREE | NUT FREE | VEGAN

A great salad dressing really elevates a simple bowl of leaves. It can also be tossed through cooled grains to form the base of a heartier salad dish. This is my simple go-to recipe.

30ml freshly squeezed **lemon juice**
100ml **olive oil** (ideally extra virgin)
1 large **garlic clove**, finely diced
½ teaspoon **sugar**
¼ teaspoon **sea salt**
Cracked black pepper

Optional addition: 1 teaspoon **wholegrain mustard**

Place all the ingredients into a jar and shake well. Taste and adjust seasoning as needed.

Will last up to three weeks in the fridge.

HONEY, BERRY & ROSEMARY SHRUB

MAKES 450ML

GLUTEN FREE | NUT FREE | VEGETARIAN

I've well and truly jumped on the shrub bandwagon. These traditional vinegar-based cordials are wonderful. There's real depth to the flavour and a pleasing tang. They're incredibly hydrating on a hot day and fantastic in both simple non-alcoholic preparations or as a mixer with spirits.

1 generous cup **fresh** or **frozen berries**
½ cup **honey**
1 cup **apple cider vinegar**
1 sprig **fresh rosemary**
Soda water to serve

Place the berries and honey in a jar and mix well, mashing the berries to break them up as much as possible. Place the lid on and leave on the kitchen bench for two days, shaking a couple of times each day. Add the apple cider vinegar and the rosemary and leave for one more day.

Use a sieve to strain the liquid from the berry and honey mix. Allow to strain for 30 minutes without pressing the fruit (this avoids sediment in your end product).

Pour the syrup into a clean jar or bottle. Top with a lid, place in the fridge and ideally leave for 1 week so that the flavours can mellow and come together.

To serve

Pour 2-3 tablespoons of the shrub into a glass filled with ice. Top with soda water.

FLAVOURED BUTTERS

GLUTEN FREE | NUT FREE | VEGETARIAN

I love butter. It makes everything taste better. Levelling up this kitchen essential of mine yields very delicious results.

I've suggested a few of my favourite flavour combinations here. The method for making each is the same.

MISO, SPRING ONION & BLACK PEPPER BUTTER

Spread this thickly on sourdough and top with avocado, melt it over steamed green vegetables or use instead of regular butter when cooking creamy scrambled eggs.

200g room temperature **butter**, cut into cubes
2 rounded tablespoons **miso paste**
1 **spring onion**, green part very finely chopped
Generous grind **cracked black pepper**

MEDJOOL DATE & SEA SALT BUTTER

Enjoy on freshly baked scones or melted over poached fruit.

200g room temperature **butter**, cut into cubes
8 **medjool dates**, finely chopped
Generous pinch **flaky sea salt**

PAPRIKA & LIME BUTTER

Wonderful on grilled chicken or barbecued corn cobs.

200g room temperature **butter**, cut into cubes
Zest of 3 **limes**
1 teaspoon good quality **hot smoked paprika**
Generous pinch **sea salt**

Method
Remove the butter from the fridge 20 minutes prior to using. Place all ingredients in a food processor and run at a medium speed until evenly mixed. Spoon into small bowls to set or lay out on a large piece of cling film or baking paper and roll into a log. Twist each end to secure. These flavoured butters will last up to four weeks in the fridge or up to three months in the freezer.

THE EASIEST ONE BOWL GLUTEN FREE PIZZA BASE

MAKE 1 LARGE BASE
DAIRY FREE (IF NON-DAIRY MILK IS USED) | GLUTEN FREE | VEGETARIAN

A simple no-knead, gluten free pizza base. You mix it up, pour it onto a tray and then bake. Suspiciously easy I know but I promise it's a winner.

1 cup **tapioca flour**
1¼ cups **almond meal**
1 teaspoon **gluten free baking powder**
½ cup **milk** (any milk is fine)
2 tablespoons **olive oil**
1 free range **egg**
¼ teaspoon **sea salt**

Preheat the oven to 220°C.

Combine all the ingredients in a bowl. Whisk until smooth. Set aside for 5 minutes. Mix again.

Pour the mixture onto a lined baking sheet. Use a spatula to spread into a circle that is roughly 30cm in diameter. Bake for 10-12 minutes until just cooked.

Place on a wire rack to cool for 10 minutes.

When you're ready to use the base, simply top with pizza sauce and all your favourite toppings.

Bake for 8-10 minutes until the cheese is bubbling.

DUKKAH

MAKES 2 CUPS
GLUTEN FREE | VEGAN

Dukkah is one of those brilliant things that once in your pantry, you'll find it can enhance lots of dishes. Of course it's hard to go past pairing it with bread and excellent olive oil, but also use this Egyptian blend over salads, with avocado, sprinkled on soup and scattered over steamed veges. It makes a really nice edible gift too because it keeps for ages.

½ cup **pistachio nuts**
½ cup **raw almonds**
2 tablespoons **coriander seeds**
2 tablespoons **fennel seeds**
1 tablespoon **cumin seeds**
¼ cup **sesame seeds**
1 teaspoon **sea salt**

Preheat the oven to 170°C. Place the nuts in an oven proof dish and roast for 10 minutes.

Heat a dry skillet over a medium-low heat. Toast the coriander seeds, fennel seeds and cumin seeds for a few minutes until fragrant. Remove from the skillet.

Wipe out the hot skillet with a dry cloth. Place the sesame seeds in the pan over the same heat. Toast for a few minutes until lightly golden.

Place the nuts and spices into a food processor. Blitz until it has the texture of coarse breadcrumbs. Stir through the sesame seeds and salt. Allow to cool completely before storing in an airtight glass jar for up to three months.

GREEN TEA INFUSED COCONUT WATER

MAKES 500MLS / SERVES 2-3
GLUTEN FREE | NUT FREE | VEGAN

This hydrating drink is a really lovely one to sip on hot and humid summer days.

3 **green tea teabags**
500mls **coconut water**
Additional **liquid sweetener** such as honey if desired

To serve: **ice**, **cucumber** slices, **fresh herbs** like **fennel fronds** or **mint leaves**

Combine the teabags and coconut water in a jug. Place in the fridge and allow to infuse for at least one hour and up to 12 hours. Add some honey if desired. Serve over ice.

NON-ALCOHOLIC WHITE SANGRIA

MAKES 1 LITRE
GLUTEN FREE | NUT FREE | VEGAN

I'm not a huge drinker at all these days and love finding drinks that are delicious and feel celebratory while leaving out the alcohol. I recently tried some 0% wines and it got me inspired to create an alcohol free spin on a white sangria. This is a yummy cocktail for a hot afternoon.

Use whatever fruit is in season and tastes great.

1 bottle chilled **non-alcoholic white wine** (I used a NZ sauvignon blanc)
½ cup **non-alcoholic spirit** (I used Seedlip Garden 108)
1 cup chilled **apple juice**
Sparkling water to top
1 **peach**, sliced
1 **apple**, sliced
1 **lime** or **lemon**, sliced
Ice as needed

Half fill a large pitcher with ice. Pour in the wine, non alcoholic spirit and juice. Top with sparkling water. Stir gently. Add the sliced fruit and stir a little more.

Serve immediately.

TURMERIC, CINNAMON & GINGER LATTE PASTE

MAKES 12 SERVES
GLUTEN FREE | NUT FREE | VEGAN

I really enjoy a turmeric latte when the weather is chilly and I'm looking for a non-caffeinated beverage that feels uplifting. I'll often make one for Luke and I in the evenings. It's so nice as part of a wind down routine at night. Making this handy paste in advance means you don't need to blend and simmer spices every time.

¼ cup **ground turmeric powder**
¼ teaspoon **freshly ground black pepper**
2 tablespoons finely grated **ginger root**
½ teaspoon **ground cinnamon**
1 cup **water**
2 teaspoons good quality **vanilla extract**
¼ cup **extra virgin coconut oil**

Combine all ingredients (except coconut oil) in a small saucepan. Whisk continuously over a medium heat until it starts bubbling. Reduce to a low heat and continue to whisk for 3-4 minutes until you have a smooth paste. Remove from the heat, add the coconut oil and whisk well. Place in a small clean glass jar. Store in the fridge for up to a month.

To make a single serve of turmeric latte

Place one teaspoon of the turmeric paste into a mug. Top with ½ cup of boiling water. Add ¾ cup of heated coconut milk. Stir briskly. Add honey to sweeten as desired.

192
Caramelised
Banana & Ginger
Upside Down Cake

194
Chocolate &
Raspberry Granola

196
Custard Two Ways

198
Creamy Honey &
Vanilla Mascarpone
Tarts with Chocolate
Almond Base

200
Chocolate
Self-Saucing Pudding
with Raspberries

202
Mexican Wedding
Cookies

204
Peanut Butter,
Banana, Chocolate &
Raspberry Loaf

206
Real Hot Chocolate
with Warming Spices

208
Apple & Brown
Sugar Galette

210
Oaty Banana,
Chocolate &
Cranberry Baked
Bliss Bites

212
Vanilla & Nutmeg
Panna Cotta with
Roasted Strawberries

214
Olive Oil, Yoghurt,
Lemon & Rosemary
Tea Cake

216
Stone Fruit &
Raspberry Clafoutis

218
Gluten Free Cornflake
& Cocoa Biscuits

220
Lemonade
Popsicles

The Sweet Stuff

CARAMELISED BANANA & GINGER UPSIDE DOWN CAKE

SERVES 8
GLUTEN FREE

This dances a line between cake and pudding. It's wonderful.

Coconut sugar is great in this with its lovely toasty flavour, but you'll get away with regular sugar if that's what you have.

2 **ripe bananas**, mashed well
3 free range **eggs**, lightly whisked
1 teaspoon **vanilla extract**
½ cup **coconut sugar**
1 rounded teaspoon **gluten free baking powder**
1 tablespoon **ground ginger**
½ teaspoon **mixed spice**
½ teaspoon **ground cinnamon**
1½ cups **almond meal**
½ cup **tapioca flour** (could also use brown rice flour or spelt flour, though that's not GF)
100g **butter**, melted

TOPPING

75g **butter**, melted
3 tablespoons **coconut sugar**
2 **ripe bananas**, each sliced into 3 long strips lengthways

Preheat the oven to 180°C.

Combine the mashed banana, egg, vanilla, sugar, baking powder, ginger, mixed spice and cinnamon in a large bowl. Mix together well. Add the almond meal and tapioca flour. Don't overmix. Finally, stir through the melted butter.

Double line a 23cm spring-form cake pan with baking paper. This is very important otherwise you may have sugary leaks into your oven which can burn and smoke. Alternatively use a 23cm cast iron skillet (line with just a single layer)

To prepare the topping, pour the melted butter into the bottom of the tin.

Sprinkle the sugar evenly over the butter. Lay the sliced bananas on the sugar and then pour over the cake batter. Use a spatula to smooth out the top.

Bake for 30-35 minutes until a skewer comes out clean when inserted. Let the cake sit for 10 minutes before inverting onto a plate. Slice and serve with fresh cream or ice cream. Leftover cake can be stored in the fridge for up to three days.

Gently reheat in the oven.

CHOCOLATE & RASPBERRY GRANOLA

MAKES 4 CUPS
VEGAN (WHEN USING COCONUT OIL)

I eat this with a big dollop of Greek or coconut yoghurt. It's lovely for gifting too.

2 cups **rolled oats**
½ cup each: **pumpkin seeds, sunflower seeds, pistachio nuts**
¼ cup each: **sesame seeds, coconut threads**
3 tablespoons **chia seeds**
3 tablespoons **cocoa powder**
½ teaspoon **ground cinnamon**
Generous pinch **salt**
60g **butter**, melted (use coconut oil for dairy free)
3 tablespoons **maple syrup**
½ cup **freeze-dried raspberries**

Preheat oven to 160°C.

Combine the oats, nuts, seeds, coconut, cocoa powder, cinnamon and salt in a large bowl. Stir to combine.

Whisk the butter or coconut oil and maple syrup together and pour over the top. Stir well to ensure the granola is evenly coated.

Lay out on a large baking sheet lined with baking paper.

Bake for 20 minutes, tossing once during the cooking, until well toasted.

Allow to cool completely before mixing through the freeze-dried raspberries.

Store in an airtight container for up to two weeks.

CUSTARD TWO WAYS

MAKES APPROX. 3 CUPS

There's nothing like proper homemade custard. It doesn't need to be overly sweet and can be whipped up in no time. We enjoy it often for dessert with fresh or cooked fruit.

DAIRY CUSTARD

GLUTEN FREE | NUT FREE | VEGETARIAN

600ml **full fat milk**
3 free range **egg yolks**
2 tablespoons **sugar**
1 tablespoon **cornflour**
1 teaspoon **vanilla extract**

Heat the milk until hot but not boiling. Whisk together the egg yolks, sugar, cornflour and vanilla.

Pour about ½ cup of the hot milk very slowly into the egg yolks and whisk briskly. Pour this all back into the hot milk pot and cook over a medium heat, whisking constantly, until it starts to simmer. Give it one minute more and then remove from the heat. Taste and adjust sweetness if desired.

NON-DAIRY CUSTARD

GLUTEN FREE | NUT FREE | VEGETARIAN

1½ cups **coconut milk** (a good rich one)
1 cup **almond milk**
1 teaspoon **vanilla extract**
3 free range **egg yolks**
2 tablespoons **sugar**
2 tablespoons **cornflour**

Heat the coconut milk, almond milk and vanilla until just before simmering. Whisk together the egg yolks, sugar and cornflour. Pour about ½ cup of the hot milk very slowly into the egg yolks and whisk really briskly. Pour this all back into the hot milk pot and cook just below simmering point, whisking constantly, for 3-4 minutes. Watch the heat as plant-based milks will split if overheated. The finished custard should be thickened and coat the back of a spoon. Taste and adjust sweetness if desired.

CREAMY HONEY & VANILLA MASCARPONE TARTS WITH CHOCOLATE ALMOND BASE

SERVES 4
GLUTEN FREE | VEGETARIAN

Make the bases a day ahead and you'll have an easy but impressive looking dessert to serve up. Ideally you'll fill and top your tarts no more than an hour before serving.

COOK'S TIP
I've made a vegan version of this dessert using either vanilla coconut yoghurt or the coconut whipping cream you can buy in a can.

CHOCOLATE ALMOND BASE
¾ cup **dried dates**
¼ cup **cocoa**
1 cup **desiccated coconut**
1½ cups **almond meal**
1 tablespoon **chia seeds**
Pinch **sea salt**

FILLING
500g **mascarpone** (remove from fridge 30 minutes prior to using)
½ cup **cream**
2 tablespoons **honey**
1 teaspoon **vanilla essence**

TOPPING
2 cups **mixed fresh berries**

Base method

Preheat oven to 160°C.

Place the dates in a bowl and cover with boiling water. Soak for 10 minutes, before draining well.

Place the cocoa, coconut, almond meal, chia seeds and salt into a food processor. Run the machine until the mixture is the texture of fine breadcrumbs. Add the dates. Blitz until roughly even in consistency and the dough sticks together when pressed between two fingers.

Grease 4 x 10cm flan dishes with removable bases.

Divide the mixture into 4 portions and press evenly and firmly into each tin. Spend a little time doing this. It will make a difference to the end result. You may not need all the mixture. Tidy the edges with a knife and prick the base a few times with a fork.

Bake for 15 minutes. Watch carefully and do not let them burn. Leave to cool completely and then remove from the tins.

Filling and topping

Place the mascarpone, cream and honey in a bowl and use an electric beater to whip together for a minute or so. Add vanilla and quickly beat to combine.

Spoon the filling into the tart cases. Top with berries close to serving.

Leftover tarts can be stored in the fridge for 24 hours.

CHOCOLATE SELF-SAUCING PUDDING WITH RASPBERRIES

SERVES 4-6
NUT FREE

The cosiest and best of the classic New Zealand puddings, in my opinion. Just wonderful with vanilla ice cream or cream.

½ cup **milk**
1 free range **egg**
½ cup **melted butter** or **coconut oil** (cooled a little)
1 cup **white spelt flour** (regular flour will work too)
2 teaspoons **baking powder**
2 tablespoons **dark cocoa powder**
⅓ cup **caster sugar**
½ cup **frozen** or **fresh raspberries** (do not thaw if using frozen)

SAUCE
1 cup **caster sugar**
3 tablespoons **dark cocoa powder**
1½ cups **boiling water**

Preheat oven to 180°C.

Whisk together the milk, egg and melted butter. In a large bowl sift the flour, baking powder and cocoa powder. Stir through the sugar.

Create a well in the middle and pour in the milk, egg and butter. Stir until well combined.

Grease an oven proof 1.5 litre capacity baking dish. Spoon the batter into the dish. It doesn't have to be smoothed out to the side. Press the raspberries evenly across the surface of the mixture.

Whisk together the sugar, cocoa and boiling water for the sauce. Carefully pour into the dish. It can be helpful to do this over the back of a large spoon to stop the boiling water disturbing the surface of the pudding batter.

Bake for 35-45 minutes until the pudding feels lightly firm and springs back when pressed.

Ideally allow it to sit for 10-15 minutes before serving.

MEXICAN WEDDING COOKIES

MAKES APPROXIMATELY 40 COOKIES
VEGETARIAN

These cookies are traditionally served and gifted around times of celebration but I will happily make and enjoy them any time of year. They are light and buttery and just exquisite. Perfect with a cup of tea.

½ cup **raw almonds**
½ cup **raw shelled pistachio nuts**
250g **butter**, room temperature
½ cup **sugar**
1 tablespoon **vanilla extract**
2¼ cups **white spelt** or **regular flour,** sifted
¼ teaspoon **salt**
1 cup **icing sugar**, for rolling cookies in

Toast the nuts on a dry skillet until lightly browned. Cool completely before placing in a food processor and blitzing until you have a rough crumb.

Place the butter and sugar in a medium sized bowl. Use an electric beater to cream together until fluffy and lighter in colour. Add the vanilla. Beat briefly.

Add the flour, salt and the ground nuts. Mix at a low speed until just combined.

Place dough in the fridge to chill for 1 hour.

Preheat the oven to 165℃.

Roll rounded teaspoons of dough into balls and place on a lined baking sheet (do not flatten).

The cookies will expand just a little so allow a little bit of space between them on the tray.

Bake for around 15 minutes until lightly golden.

Remove from the oven and leave to cool for a few minutes before transferring to a wire rack.

Roll in icing sugar while still warm (not hot). Once cooled completely, store in an airtight container for up to two weeks.

PEANUT BUTTER, BANANA, CHOCOLATE & RASPBERRY LOAF

DAIRY FREE | GLUTEN FREE | VEGETARIAN

This loaf makes a fantastic breakfast, lunch box filler or afternoon snack. The versatile batter can also be used to make muffins or even a cake. Baking times for these other options are listed below the recipe.

2 **ripe bananas**, peeled and sliced
4 free range **eggs**
½ cup **peanut butter** (I prefer to use smooth)
½ cup **sugar** (coconut sugar is lovely in this)
2½ cups **almond meal**
⅓ cup **tapioca flour**
2 teaspoons **vanilla essence**
¾ teaspoon **baking soda**
1 teaspoon **apple cider vinegar**
100g **dairy free dark chocolate**, roughly chopped
1 cup **frozen** or **fresh raspberries** (do not thaw beforehand if using frozen)

Preheat oven to 160℃

Place the bananas, eggs, peanut butter, sugar and half the almond meal into a food processor. Blend until smooth. Add the rest of the almond meal, flour, vanilla essence, baking soda and apple cider vinegar. Combine well.

Remove the blade from the food processor and gently stir through the chocolate with a spoon.

Pour mixture into a 23cm loaf tin that has been well greased or lined.

Gently press the raspberries into the top of the batter.

Bake for around 60 minutes until golden and a skewer comes out clean when inserted. Wait until the loaf is completely cool before slicing.

Will last four days in an airtight container in the fridge.

To make 12 regular-sized muffins: bake for 20-30 minutes

To make a cake in a 23cm tin: bake for 50-60 minutes

REAL HOT CHOCOLATE WITH WARMING SPICES

SERVES 3-4

GLUTEN FREE | VEGAN (IF NON DAIRY SUBSTITUTION USED)

This is SO rich and a really lovely option for a warming dessert drink. If you use a good quality dark chocolate, you'll also find it not too sweet.

3 cups **plant-based milk** (I like a 50/50 blend of coconut and almond milk) or 3 cups **dairy milk**

¼ teaspoon **ground cinnamon**

Generous pinch **ground nutmeg**

Pinch **cayenne pepper** (optional)

100g good quality **dark chocolate**, finely chopped

Heat your milk, cinnamon, nutmeg and cayenne pepper until hot but not boiling. There should be little bubbles around the outside of the pot. Add the chocolate and whisk briskly until silky smooth.

Serve immediately in mugs.

Leftovers can be whisked together to correct any separation and then gently reheated.

APPLE & BROWN SUGAR GALETTE

SERVE 4-6
NUT FREE | VEGETARIAN

On the day I shot this recipe, it was the perfect use for a bag of apples that turned out to be too floury. The pastry is easy to make and the pie is formed by simply folding the pastry around the sliced fruit. It's meant to be rustic so don't obsess over the form too much.

Serve with a drizzle of cream or with ice cream.

90g **cold butter**, cut into cubes
1½ cups **spelt flour** or plain flour
2 tablespoons **caster sugar**
1 free range **egg**, whisked lightly
5 medium **apples**, peeled and sliced
Juice of 1 **lemon**
½ teaspoon **ground cinnamon**
3 tablespoons **brown sugar**
1 rounded tablespoon **cornflour** or **tapioca flour**
Icing sugar for dusting

Place the butter, flour and sugar into a food processor and pulse until the texture resembles coarse breadcrumbs. Add the egg and pulse to bring together into a ball.

Place in the fridge to chill for 30 minutes.

Preheat the oven to 180°C.

Place the apple in a bowl with the lemon juice, cinnamon, sugar and cornflour. Toss to coat evenly.

Take the dough from the fridge and place on a large piece of baking paper. Roll out until roughly circular and 35 cm in diameter. Move onto an oven proof tray with baking paper still underneath. Place the fruit on top leaving roughly 7-8 cm around the edges.

Place your hands under the baking paper and fold the pastry over the fruit. It doesn't need to be perfect. Patch up any cracks in the pastry if needed

Bake for 40 minutes until the pastry is golden. Sprinkle with icing sugar and cool for 15-20 minutes before serving.

OATY BANANA, CHOCOLATE & CRANBERRY BAKED BLISS BITES

MAKES 12 BALLS
NUT FREE | VEGAN

These have the best texture, crunchy on the outside and soft in the middle. Fantastic for lunchboxes (for young and old) or with a cup of tea.

1 **ripe banana**, mashed
1½ cups **rolled oats**
¼ cup **sugar** (any type will work)
2 tablespoons **chia seeds**
¼ cup **melted coconut oil**
1 teaspoon **vanilla extract**
⅓ cup **dairy free dark chocolate chips**
½ cup **dried cranberries**

Preheat the oven to 180℃.

Combine the banana, rolled oats, sugar, chia seeds, coconut oil and vanilla in a large bowl. Use a fork to mash it all together until well mixed. Add the chocolate chips and cranberries and mix until evenly dispersed.

Leave the mixture to sit for 5 minutes in the fridge.

Use wet hands (this is essential) and a firm touch to form heaped tablespoons of the mixture into balls. Place onto a lined oven proof tray. Bake for 15 minutes, until lightly golden.

Allow to cool completely before storing in an airtight container for up to five days. Will freeze well for up to two months.

VANILLA & NUTMEG PANNA COTTA WITH ROASTED STRAWBERRIES

SERVES 6
GLUTEN FREE | NUT FREE

Roasting transforms strawberries in the most wonderful way. They become rich and intense. Combined with panna cotta they make a lovely, simple dessert, one of my all time favourites.

You can prepare this whole recipe the day before you serve it, making it a nice choice for entertaining. To avoid the silly stress of trying to get the panna cotta out of the moulds perfectly, I simply serve it in small glasses. Much less fuss.

1 tablespoon **powdered gelatin**
1½ cups **milk**
2 cups **cream**
¼ cup **caster sugar**
¼ teaspoon **ground nutmeg**
1 teaspoon **vanilla extract**
2 punnets of **strawberries**, trimmed and halved
2 tablespoons **pure maple syrup**
1 tablespoon **balsamic vinegar**

Mix the gelatin with ½ cup of milk in a small bowl. Leave this for 5 minutes to 'bloom'.

Place the remaining milk in a medium saucepan along with the cream, sugar, nutmeg and vanilla. Heat until very hot but not bubbling.

Add the soaked gelatin mixture and whisk until smooth. Leave to cool until just warm. Give it another quick whisk.

Pour into six small glasses. Place in the fridge to set (about four hours).

Preheat the oven to 180°C.

Toss the strawberries with the maple syrup and vinegar until evenly coated. Place in an ovenproof dish and cook for 25 minutes. Leave to cool completely.

Spoon some of the strawberries into each glass just before serving.

OLIVE OIL, YOGHURT, LEMON & ROSEMARY TEA CAKE

GLUTEN FREE (IF SUBSTITUTION IS USED) | VEGETARIAN

I have a fairly restrained sweet tooth and this cake really hits the spot for me. Hints of rich olive oil and fragrant rosemary alongside lovely soft sweetness. I much prefer a drizzle of icing rather than a thick layer. This makes a wonderful morning snack with a cup of tea.

4 free range **eggs**
½ cup **extra virgin olive oil**
½ cup **full fat Greek yoghurt**
½ cup **sugar**
2 teaspoons **vanilla essence**
Zest of 1 **lemon**
1 tablespoon finely chopped **rosemary leaves**
2½ cups **almond meal**
¼ cup **white spelt flour** (**regular flour** will work or **brown rice flour** to make it gluten free)
1 teaspoon **baking powder** (use gluten free if needed)

ICING

1½ cups **icing sugar**
3-4 tablespoons **lemon juice**

To garnish: **dried rose petals** (optional)

Preheat oven to 160°C

Whisk together the eggs, olive oil, yoghurt, sugar, vanilla, lemon zest and rosemary.

Add the almond meal, flour and baking powder. Stir to combine.

Pour the batter into a lined or well greased cake tin.

Bake for 45-50 minutes until lightly golden and a skewer comes out clean when inserted.

Cool cake completely before mixing together the icing and drizzling over the cake. Sprinkle with rose petals if using.

STONE FRUIT AND RASPBERRY CLAFOUTIS

SERVES 4
GLUTEN FREE (IF SUBSTITUTION USED) | NUT FREE | VEGETARIAN

This is the easiest dessert ever and an absolute delight. A french classic that can be whipped up and in the oven in 10 minutes. The day that I ended up shooting this recipe for my book, I threw it all together at 4.30 in the afternoon after spotting some peaches and nectarines on my kitchen windowsill that had to be used. I photographed it, then made us dinner and it was perfectly warm when we had it for dessert later.

I make this recipe with all kinds of fruit so use whatever you have on hand. Cherries, rhubarb and pears are all fantastic.

½ cup **flour** (regular or **gluten free all-purpose** will both work well)
½ teaspoon **baking powder** (use gluten free baking powder if needed)
½ cup **sugar**
Pinch **salt**
3 free range **eggs**
1 cup **full fat milk**
½ cup **cream**
1½ teaspoons **vanilla extract**
2 **nectarines** or **peaches**, stone removed and sliced fairly thinly
Handful **fresh** or **frozen raspberries**

To serve: **icing sugar** for dusting, **fresh cream**

Preheat the oven to 180°C.

Place the flour, baking powder, sugar and salt in a large bowl. Whisk briefly to combine.

Add the eggs, milk, cream and vanilla. Whisk until very smooth.

Pour into a well greased 23cm round dish. I like to use a cast iron pan or heavy-bottomed pie dish. Tile the sliced fruit on top. The pieces can overlap. Dot the raspberries over this.

Bake for 30-35 minutes until lightly golden and mostly set. A little quiver in the middle is fine.

Allow to cool until just warm. Dust with icing sugar and serve with fresh cream.

GLUTEN FREE CORNFLAKE & COCOA BISCUITS

MAKES 18 BISCUITS
GLUTEN FREE | VEGETARIAN

My gluten free version of that classic New Zealand treat (my favourite biscuit) is delicious and easy.

200g room temperature **butter**
½ cup **brown sugar**
⅓ cup **dark cocoa powder**
¾ cup **almond meal**
1 cup **tapioca flour**
2½ cups **gluten free cornflakes**

CHOCOLATE ICING
1½ cups **icing sugar**
2-3 tablespoons **dark cocoa powder**
1-2 tablespoons **boiling water**, as needed

Preheat the oven to 180°C.

Cream the butter and sugar until light and fluffy. Mix the cocoa powder, almond meal and tapioca flour together quickly in a separate bowl and add to the butter and sugar. Use a spatula to help combine this. Mix in the cornflakes. It may take a minute or so to bring it all together.

Use damp hands to roll rounded tablespoons of mixture into balls and then flatten into a chunky biscuit shape with two fingers or the heel of your hand. Place onto a lined baking tray.

Bake for 12-15 minutes.

Cool biscuits completely before mixing together the icing sugar and cocoa powder. Add water carefully until you've got a very thick but spreadable consistency. Spread a little onto each biscuit. Store in an airtight container.

LEMONADE POPSICLES

MAKES 6 ICE BLOCKS
GLUTEN FREE | NUT FREE | VEGAN

When I showed my daughters the images for this chapter and asked them what they thought I was missing, Bonnie suggested a classic lemonade popsicle recipe would finish things up nicely. I think she was right. These are just the clean and bright treats we need on a sunny autumn afternoon when our citrus trees are loaded with fruit.

⅓ cup **fresh lemon juice** (lime is also great)
¾ cup **icing sugar**
1½ cups **water**

Whisk the lemon juice and sugar together until the sugar is almost dissolved. Add the water and whisk well.

Pour into ice block moulds. Freeze for 6-8 hours until solid.

INDEX

A

A Late Spring Vegetable & White Bean Soup 36

A Very Simple (And Quite Perfect) Mushroom Soup 54

Apple & Brown Sugar Galette 208

Asparagus

A Late Spring Vegetable & White Bean Soup 36

Honey & Spice Roasted Vegetable Salad with Honey Tahini Dressing 38

Avocado

Black Bean Salad with Coriander & Honey Dressing 28

Breakfast For Dinner Pizza 80

Hummus & Haloumi Salad 52

Everyday Green Salad 56

Spiced Fish Tacos with Pickle & Caper Mayo 70

Tortilla Soup 46

B

Banana

Caramelised Banana & Ginger Upside Down Cake 192

Oaty Banana, Chocolate & Cranberry Baked Bliss Bites 210

Peanut Butter, Banana, Chocolate & Raspberry Loaf 204

Barbecued Vegetable Salad with Chive & Garlic Yoghurt 42

Beans

A Late Spring Vegetable & White Bean Soup 36

Black Bean Salad with Coriander & Honey Dressing 28

Bonnie's Smoky Baked Beans 66

Everyday Green Salad 56

Tortilla Soup 46

Beef

Beef & Mushroom Stew with Cheddar & Parsley Dumplings 108

Mexican Spiced Beef Cheeks with Coriander & Jalapeno Sauce 110

Smash Burgers with The Best Burger Sauce 68

Soy, Ginger & Sesame Rump Steak 88

Beef & Mushroom Stew with Cheddar & Parsley Dumplings 108

Beetroot Cured Salmon with Lemon & Caper Cream 154

Black Bean Salad with Coriander & Honey Dressing 28

Bonnie's Smoky Baked Beans 66

Breakfast For Dinner Pizza 80

Broccoli

Broccoli & Cheese Fritters with Garlic & Mint Yoghurt 144

Broccoli & Greens Tart with Buckwheat & Brown Rice Crust 124

Chicken Noodle Soup 40

Kimchi Noodles 92

Thai Broccoli, Spinach & Coconut Soup 20

Broccoli & Cheese Fritters with Garlic & Mint Yoghurt 144

Broccoli & Greens Tart with Buckwheat & Brown Rice Crust 124

Broth

Chicken Broth 162

Buckwheat

Broccoli & Greens Tart with Buckwheat & Brown Rice Crust 124

Buckwheat, Silverbeet, Cranberries & Rosemary with Creamy Hummus 32

C

Cabbage

Sautéed Red Cabbage with Apple Cider Vinegar 15

Capsicum

Barbecued Vegetable Salad with Chive & Garlic Yoghurt 42

Black Bean Salad with Coriander & Honey Dressing 28

Honey & Spice Roasted Vegetable Salad with Honey Tahini Dressing 38

Spanish Style Chicken Tray Bake 76

Caramelised Banana & Ginger Upside Down Cake 192

Carrots

Everything Soup 50

Honey & Spice Roasted Vegetable Salad with Honey Tahini Dressing 38

Moroccan Quinoa, Chickpea & Hemp Seed Salad 34

Cauliflower

Fried Cauliflower Rice with Crispy Fried Eggs 84

Greek Cauliflower, Olive & Chickpea Stew 78

Honey & Spice Roasted Vegetable Salad with Honey Tahini Dressing 38

Moroccan Lamb Lasagne with Cauliflower Béchamel 106

Turmeric Roasted Cauliflower with Dates, Pistachios, Mint & Lemon 30

Chicken

Chicken Broth 162

Chicken, Mushroom & Black Pepper Wonton Soup 100

Chicken Noodle Soup 40

Creamy Chicken, Chickpea & Spinach Curry 112

Mum's Schnitzel 82

Red Curry Roasted Chicken 72

Roast Chicken & Sourdough 118

Spanish Style Chicken Tray Bake 76

Vietnamese Inspired Chicken Lettuce Cups 90

Chicken Broth 162

Chicken, Mushroom & Black Pepper Wonton Soup 100

Chicken Noodle Soup 40

Chickpeas

Buckwheat, Silverbeet, Cranberries & Rosemary with Creamy Hummus 32

Creamy Chicken, Chickpea & Spinach Curry 112

Greek Cauliflower, Olive & Chickpea Stew 78

Honey & Spice Roasted Vegetable Salad with Honey Tahini Dressing 38

Hummus & Haloumi Salad 52

Moroccan Quinoa, Chickpea & Hemp Seed Salad 34

Roast Chicken & Sourdough 118

Tortilla Soup 46

Chilli & Garlic Oil 170

Chocolate

Chocolate & Raspberry Granola 194

Chocolate Self-Saucing Pudding with Raspberries 200

Creamy Honey & Vanilla Mascarpone Tarts with Chocolate Almond Base 198

Oaty Banana, Chocolate & Cranberry Baked Bliss Bites 210

Peanut Butter, Banana, Chocolate & Raspberry Loaf 204

Real Hot Chocolate with Warming Spices 206

Chocolate & Raspberry Granola 194

Chocolate Self-Saucing Pudding with Raspberries 200

Chorizo

New Potato Salad with Crispy Chorizo, Olives, Green Beans & Lemon Mayo 22

Red Lentil, Chorizo, Rosemary & Lemon Soup 26

Coconut

Thai Broccoli, Spinach & Coconut Soup 20

Coriander & Jalapeno Sauce 110

Courgettes

A Late Spring Vegetable & White Bean Soup 36

Barbecued Vegetable Salad with Chive & Garlic Yoghurt 42

Chicken Noodle Soup 40

Everything Soup 50

Honey & Spice Roasted Vegetable Salad with Honey Tahini Dressing 38

Creamy Chicken, Chickpea & Spinach Curry 112

Creamy Garlic Mushrooms 140

Creamy Honey & Vanilla Mascarpone Tarts with Chocolate Almond Base 198

Custard

Custard Two Ways 196

Dairy Custard 196

Non Dairy Custard 196

D

Dairy Free

Chicken, Mushroom & Black Pepper Wonton Soup 100

Creamy Garlic Mushrooms 140

Moroccan Lamb Lasagne with Cauliflower Béchamel 106

Peanut Butter, Banana, Chocolate & Raspberry Loaf 204

The Easiest One Bowl Gluten Free Pizza Base 178

Dressing

Basil Dressing 24

Caesar Salad 44

Coriander & Honey Dressing 28

Honey Tahini Dressing 38

One Minute Mayo 168

Pickle & Caper Mayo 70

Tahini Miso Dressing 18

The Dressing For Everything 172

Dukkah 180

E

Easy Flaxseed Crackers 132

Egg
   The Best Egg Salad 146

Eggplant
   Barbecued Vegetable Salad with Chive & Garlic Yoghurt 42

Everyday Green Salad 56

Everything Soup 50

F

Fancy Kiwi Onion Dip 142

Fish
   Beetroot Cured Salmon with Lemon & Caper Cream 154
   Kedgeree with Smoked Salmon & Dill 98
   Kelly's Fish Pie 102
   Potted Smoked Fish with Lemon, Horseradish & Dill 148
   Spiced Fish Tacos with Pickle & Caper Mayo 70

Flavoured Butters
   Miso, Spring Onion & Black Pepper Butter 176
   Medjool Date & Sea Salt Butter 176
   Paprika & Lime Butter 176

Fried Cauliflower Rice with Crispy Fried Eggs 84

G

Gluten Free
   A Late Spring Vegetable & White Bean Soup 36
   A Very Simple (And Quite Perfect) Mushroom Soup 54
   Barbecued Vegetable Salad with Chive & Garlic Yoghurt 42
   Beetroot Cured Salmon with Lemon & Caper Cream 154
   Black Bean Salad with Coriander & Honey Dressing 28

Bonnie's Smoky Baked Beans 66

Breakfast For Dinner Pizza 80

Broccoli & Cheese Fritters with Garlic & Mint Yoghurt 144

Broccoli & Greens Tart with Buckwheat & Brown Rice Crust 124

Buckwheat, Silverbeet, Cranberries & Rosemary with Creamy Hummus 32

Caramelised Banana & Ginger Upside Down Cake 192

Chicken Broth 162

Chicken Noodle Soup 40

Chilli & Garlic Oil 170

Creamy Chicken, Chickpea & Spinach Curry 112

Creamy Garlic Mushrooms 140

Creamy Honey & Vanilla Mascarpone Tarts with Chocolate Almond Base 198

Dairy Custard 196

Dukkah 180

Easy Flaxseed Crackers 132

Everyday Green Salad 56

Everything Soup 50

Fancy Kiwi Onion Dip 142

Flavoured Butters 176

Fried Cauliflower Rice with Crispy Fried Eggs 84

Gluten Free Cornflake & Cocoa Biscuits 218

Grain-Free Flatbreads 110

Greek Cauliflower, Olive & Chickpea Stew 78

Green Risotto 116

Green Tea Infused Coconut Water 182

Honey & Spice Roasted Vegetable Salad with Honey Tahini Dressing 38

Honey, Berry & Rosemary Shrub 174

Hummus & Haloumi Salad 52

Iceberg Wedge Salad with Tahini Miso Dressing 18

Kedgeree with Smoked Salmon & Dill 98

Kimchi Noodles 92

Lemonade Popsicles 220

Mexican Spiced Beef Cheeks with Coriander & Jalapeno Sauce 110

Moroccan Quinoa, Chickpea & Hemp Seed Salad 34

New Potato Salad with Crispy Chorizo, Olives, Green Beans & Lemon Mayo 22

Non-Alcoholic White Sangria 184

Non-Dairy Custard 196

Okonomiyaki 104

Olive Oil, Yoghurt, Lemon & Rosemary Tea Cake 214

One Minute Mayo 168

Peanut Butter, Banana, Chocolate & Raspberry Loaf 204

Pork & Quinoa Meatballs with Turmeric Broth 58

Potted Smoked Fish with Lemon, Horseradish & Dill 148

Puy Lentils & Baby Mozzarella with Basil Dressing & Roasted Cherry Tomatoes 24

Quinoa, Spring Onion & Parmesan Patties 130

Real Hot Chocolate with Warming Spices 206

Red Curry Roasted Chicken 72

Red Lentil, Chorizo, Rosemary & Lemon Soup 26

Sautéed Red Cabbage with Apple Cider Vinegar 152

Soy, Ginger & Sesame Rump Steak 88

Spanish Style Chicken Tray Bake 76

Spiced Fish Tacos with Pickle & Caper Mayo 70

Spiced Potato Frittata with Fried Onions, Coriander & Kasundi 86

Spiced Slow Roasted Lamb Leg with Fresh Herb Sauce & Pomegranate Seeds 120

Stone Fruit And Raspberry Clafoutis 216

Thai Broccoli, Spinach & Coconut Soup 20

The Best Egg Salad 146

The Dressing For Everything 172

The Easiest One Bowl Gluten Free Pizza Base 178

Toasted Seeds 164

Tortilla Soup 46

Turmeric & Ginger Lentils 64

Turmeric, Cinnamon & Ginger Latte Paste 186

Turmeric Roasted Cauliflower with Dates, Pistachios, Mint & Lemon 30

Vanilla & Nutmeg Panna Cotta with Roasted Strawberries 212

Vegan Tray Bake Nachos with Tofu, Mushrooms & Lentil Chilli 122

Very Crunchy Roast Potatoes 150

Vietnamese Inspired Chicken Lettuce Cups 90

Gluten Free Cornflake & Cocoa Biscuits 218

Grain-Free Flatbreads 110

Greek Cauliflower, Olive & Chickpea Stew 78

Green Risotto 116

Green Tea Infused Coconut Water 182

Grilled Caesar Salad 44

H

Halloumi

Hummus & Haloumi Salad 52

Herb Sauce 120

Honey & Spice Roasted Vegetable Salad with Honey Tahini Dressing 38

Honey, Berry & Rosemary Shrub 174

Hummus 32

Hummus & Haloumi Salad 52

I

Iceberg Wedge Salad with Tahini Miso Dressing 18

K

Kedgeree with Smoked Salmon & Dill 98

Kelly's Fish Pie 102

Kimchi Noodles 92

L

Lamb

Moroccan Lamb Lasagne with Cauliflower Béchamel 106

Spiced Slow Roasted Lamb Leg with Fresh Herb Sauce & Pomegranate Seeds 120

Leeks

A Late Spring Vegetable & White Bean Soup 36

Lemonade Popsicles 220

Lentils

Everything Soup 50

Puy Lentils & Baby Mozzarella with Basil Dressing & Roasted Cherry Tomatoes 24

Red Lentil, Chorizo, Rosemary & Lemon Soup 26

Rich Mushroom & French Lentil Pie with Crunchy Filo Topping 114

Turmeric & Ginger Lentils 64

Vegan Tray Bake Nachos with Tofu, Mushrooms & Lentil Chilli 122

Lettuce

Iceberg Wedge Salad with Tahini Miso Dressing 18

M

Mayonnaise

One Minute Mayo 168

Mexican Spiced Beef Cheeks with Coriander & Jalapeno Sauce 110

Mexican Wedding Cookies 202

Miso

Iceberg Wedge Salad with Tahini Miso Dressing 18

Moroccan Lamb Lasagne with Cauliflower Béchamel 106

Moroccan Quinoa, Chickpea & Hemp Seed Salad 34

Mozzarella

Breakfast For Dinner Pizza 80

Puy Lentils & Baby Mozzarella with Basil Dressing & Roasted Cherry Tomatoes 24

Roasted Vine Tomatoes, Sourdough, Fresh Mozzarella And Green Olives 48

Mum's Schnitzel 82

Mushroom

A Very Simple (And Quite Perfect) Mushroom Soup 54

Beef & Mushroom Stew with Cheddar & Parsley Dumplings 108

Chicken, Mushroom & Black Pepper Wonton Soup 100

Creamy Garlic Mushrooms 140

Rich Mushroom & French Lentil Pie with Crunchy Filo Topping 114

Vegan Tray Bake Nachos with Tofu, Mushrooms & Lentil Chilli 122

N

New Potato Salad with Crispy Chorizo, Olives, Green Beans & Lemon Mayo 22

Non-Alcoholic White Sangria 184

Nut Free

A Late Spring Vegetable & White Bean Soup 36

A Very Simple (And Quite Perfect) Mushroom Soup 54

Apple & Brown Sugar Galette 208

Barbecued Vegetable Salad with Chive & Garlic Yoghurt 42

Beef & Mushroom Stew with Cheddar & Parsley Dumplings 108

Beetroot Cured Salmon with Lemon & Caper Cream 154

Black Bean Salad with Coriander & Honey Dressing 28

Bonnie's Smoky Baked Beans 66

Breakfast For Dinner Pizza 80

Broccoli & Cheese Fritters with Garlic & Mint Yoghurt 144

Broccoli & Greens Tart with Buckwheat & Brown Rice Crust 124

Buckwheat, Silverbeet, Cranberries & Rosemary with Creamy Hummus 32

Chicken Broth 162

Chicken Noodle Soup 40

Chilli & Garlic Oil 170

Chocolate Self-Saucing Pudding with Raspberries 200

Creamy Chicken, Chickpea & Spinach Curry 112

Creamy Garlic Mushrooms 140

Easy Flaxseed Crackers 132

Everyday Green Salad 56

Fancy Kiwi Onion Dip 142

Everything Soup 50

Flavoured Butters 176

Greek Cauliflower, Olive & Chickpea Stew 78

Green Risotto 116

Green Tea Infused Coconut Water 182

Grilled Caesar Salad 44

Honey & Spice Roasted Vegetable Salad with Honey Tahini Dressing 38

Honey, Berry & Rosemary Shrub 174

Hummus & Haloumi Salad 52

Iceberg Wedge Salad with Tahini Miso Dressing 18

Kedgeree with Smoked Salmon & Dill 98

Kelly's Fish Pie 102

Kimchi Noodles 92

Lemonade Popsicles 220

Moroccan Lamb Lasagne with Cauliflower Béchamel 106

Mum's Schnitzel 82

New Potato Salad with Crispy Chorizo, Olives, Green Beans & Lemon Mayo 22

Non-Alcoholic White Sangria 184

Oaty Banana, Chocolate & Cranberry Baked Bliss Bites 210

Okonomiyaki 104

One Minute Mayo 168

Panko-Crumbed Tofu Fingers with Spicy Mayo 138

Pork & Quinoa Meatballs with Turmeric Broth 58

Potted Smoked Fish with Lemon, Horseradish & Dill 148

Puy Lentils & Baby Mozzarella with Basil Dressing & Roasted Cherry Tomatoes 24

Quinoa, Spring Onion & Parmesan Patties 130

Red Curry Roasted Chicken 72

Red Lentil, Chorizo, Rosemary & Lemon Soup 26

Roast Chicken & Sourdough 118

Roasted Vine Tomatoes, Sourdough, Fresh Mozzarella And Green Olives 48

Sautéed Red Cabbage with Apple Cider Vinegar 152

Seedy Yoghurt Flatbreads 166

Smash Burgers with The Best Burger Sauce 68

Sourdough Stuffing with Bacon, Celery & Apple 156

Soy, Ginger & Sesame Rump Steak 88

Spaghetti Aglio Olio E Peperoncino 74

Spelt Scones with Two Cheeses & Spinach 134

Spanish Style Chicken Tray Bake 76

Spiced Fish Tacos with Pickle & Caper Mayo 70

Spiced Potato Frittata with Fried Onions, Coriander & Kasundi 86

Spiced Slow Roasted Lamb Leg with Fresh Herb Sauce & Pomegranate Seeds 120

Stone Fruit And Raspberry Clafoutis 216

The Best Egg Salad 146

The Dressing For Everything 172

Thai Broccoli, Spinach & Coconut Soup 20

Toasted Seeds 164

Tortilla Soup 46

Turmeric & Ginger Lentils 64

Turmeric, Cinnamon & Ginger Latte Paste 186

Vanilla & Nutmeg Panna Cotta with Roasted Strawberries 212

Very Crunchy Roast Potatoes 150

Vietnamese Inspired Chicken Lettuce Cups 90

O

Oaty Banana, Chocolate & Cranberry Baked Bliss Bites 210

Okonomiyaki 104

Olive Oil, Yoghurt, Lemon & Rosemary Tea Cake 214

One Minute Mayo 168

P

Panko-Crumbed Tofu Fingers with Spicy Mayo 138

Pasta

Spaghetti Aglio Olio E Peperoncino 74

Peanut Butter, Banana, Chocolate & Raspberry Loaf 204

Pork

Pork & Quinoa Meatballs with Turmeric Broth 58

Potato

New Potato Salad with Crispy Chorizo, Olives, Green Beans & Lemon Mayo 22

Spanish Style Chicken Tray Bake 76

Spiced Potato Frittata with Fried Onions, Coriander & Kasundi 86

Very Crunchy Roast Potatoes 150

Potted Smoked Fish with Lemon, Horseradish & Dill 148

Puy Lentils & Baby Mozzarella with Basil Dressing & Roasted Cherry Tomatoes 24

Q

Quinoa

Moroccan Quinoa, Chickpea & Hemp Seed Salad 34

Pork & Quinoa Meatballs with Turmeric Broth 58

Quinoa, Spring Onion & Parmesan Patties 130

R

Raspberry

Chocolate & Raspberry Granola 194

Chocolate Self-Saucing Pudding with Raspberries 200

Peanut Butter, Banana, Chocolate & Raspberry Loaf 204

Stone Fruit And Raspberry Clafoutis 216

Real Hot Chocolate with Warming Spices 206

Red Curry Roasted Chicken 72

Red Lentil, Chorizo, Rosemary & Lemon Soup 26

Rice

Green Risotto 116

Rich Mushroom & French Lentil Pie with Crunchy Filo Topping 114

Roast Chicken & Sourdough 118

Roasted Vine Tomatoes, Sourdough, Fresh Mozarella And Green Olives 48

S

Salad

Barbecued Vegetable Salad with Chive & Garlic Yoghurt 42

Black Bean Salad with Coriander & Honey Dressing 28

Buckwheat, Silverbeet, Cranberries & Rosemary with Creamy Hummus 32

Everyday Green Salad 56

Grilled Caesar Salad 44

Honey & Spice Roasted Vegetable Salad with Honey Tahini Dressing 38

Hummus & Haloumi Salad 52

Iceberg Wedge Salad with Tahini Miso Dressing 18

New Potato Salad with Crispy Chorizo, Olives, Green Beans & Lemon Mayo 22

Moroccan Quinoa, Chickpea & Hemp Seed Salad 34

Puy Lentils & Baby Mozzarella with Basil Dressing & Roasted Cherry Tomatoes 24

Roasted Vine Tomatoes, Sourdough, Fresh Mozzarella And Green Olives 48

The Best Egg Salad 146

Turmeric Roasted Cauliflower with Dates, Pistachios, Mint & Lemon 30

Sautéed Red Cabbage with Apple Cider Vinegar 152

Seedy Yoghurt Flatbreads 166

Silverbeet

Buckwheat, Silverbeet, Cranberries & Rosemary with Creamy Hummus 32

Smash Burgers with The Best Burger Sauce 68

Soup

A Late Spring Vegetable & White Bean Soup 36

A Very Simple (And Quite Perfect) Mushroom Soup 54

Chicken, Mushroom & Black Pepper Wonton Soup 100

Chicken Noodle Soup 40

Everything Soup 50

Red Lentil, Chorizo, Rosemary & Lemon Soup 26

Thai Broccoli, Spinach & Coconut Soup 20

Tortilla Soup 46

Sourdough Stuffing with Bacon, Celery & Apple 156

Soy, Ginger & Sesame Rump Steak 88

Spaghetti Aglio Olio E Peperoncino 74

Spanish Style Chicken Tray Bake 76

Spelt Scones with Two Cheeses & Spinach 134

Spiced Fish Tacos with Pickle & Caper Mayo 70

Spiced Potato Frittata with Fried Onions, Coriander & Kasundi 86

Spiced Slow Roasted Lamb Leg with Fresh Herb Sauce & Pomegranate Seeds 120

Spinach

Creamy Chicken, Chickpea & Spinach Curry 112

Spelt Scones with Two Cheeses & Spinach 134

Thai Broccoli, Spinach & Coconut Soup 20

Strawberries

Vanilla & Nutmeg Panna Cotta with Roasted Strawberries 212

Stone Fruit And Raspberry Clafoutis 216

T

Tahini

Iceberg Wedge Salad with Tahini Miso Dressing 18

Thai Broccoli, Spinach & Coconut Soup 20

The Best Egg Salad 146

The Dressing For Everything 172

The Easiest One Bowl Gluten Free Pizza Base 178

Toasted Seeds 164

Tofu

Panko-Crumbed Tofu Fingers with Spicy Mayo 138

Vegan Tray Bake Nachos with Tofu, Mushrooms & Lentil Chilli 122

Tomatoes

Bonnie's Smoky Baked Beans 66

Everything Soup 50

Greek Cauliflower, Olive & Chickpea Stew 78

Puy Lentils & Baby Mozzarella with Basil Dressing & Roasted Cherry Tomatoes 24

Red Lentil, Chorizo, Rosemary & Lemon Soup   26

Roasted Vine Tomatoes, Sourdough, Fresh Mozzarella And Green Olives   48

Spanish Style Chicken Tray Bake   76

Tortilla Soup   46

Turmeric & Ginger Lentils   64

Tortilla Soup   46

Turmeric & Ginger Lentils   64

Turmeric, Cinnamon & Ginger Latte Paste   186

Turmeric Roasted Cauliflower with Dates, Pistachios, Mint & Lemon   30

V

Vanilla & Nutmeg Panna Cotta with Roasted Strawberries   212

Vegan

A Very Simple (And Quite Perfect) Mushroom Soup   54

Bonnie's Smoky Baked Beans   66

Buckwheat, Silverbeet, Cranberries & Rosemary with Creamy Hummus   32

Chilli & Garlic Oil   170

Chocolate & Raspberry Granola   194

Creamy Garlic Mushrooms   140

Dukkah   180

Easy Flaxseed Crackers   132

Everyday Green Salad   56

Everything Soup   50

Fried Cauliflower Rice with Crispy Fried Eggs   84

Greek Cauliflower, Olive & Chickpea Stew   78

Green Tea Infused Coconut Water   182

Iceberg Wedge Salad with Tahini Miso Dressing   18

Lemonade Popsicles   220

Moroccan Quinoa, Chickpea & Hemp Seed Salad   34

Non-Alcoholic White Sangria   184

Non-Dairy Custard   196

Oaty Banana, Chocolate & Cranberry Baked Bliss Bites   210

Real Hot Chocolate with Warming Spices   206

Sautéed Red Cabbage with Apple Cider Vinegar   152

Spaghetti Aglio Olio E Peperoncino   74

Thai Broccoli, Spinach & Coconut Soup   20

The Dressing For Everything   172

Toasted Seeds   164

Tortilla Soup   46

Turmeric & Ginger Lentils   64

Turmeric, Cinnamon & Ginger Latte Paste   186

Turmeric Roasted Cauliflower with Dates, Pistachios, Mint & Lemon   30

Vegan Tray Bake Nachos with Tofu, Mushrooms & Lentil Chilli   122

Very Crunchy Roast Potatoes   150

Vegan Tray Bake Nachos with Tofu, Mushrooms & Lentil Chilli   122

Vegetarian

A Late Spring Vegetable & White Bean Soup   36

Apple & Brown Sugar Galette   208

Barbecued Vegetable Salad with Chive & Garlic Yoghurt   42

Black Bean Salad with Coriander & Honey Dressing   28

Broccoli & Cheese Fritters with Garlic & Mint Yoghurt   144

Broccoli & Greens Tart with Buckwheat & Brown Rice Crust   124

Creamy Honey & Vanilla Mascarpone Tarts with Chocolate Almond Base   198

Dairy Custard   196

Flavoured Butters   176

Gluten Free Cornflake & Cocoa Biscuits   218

Green Risotto   116

Honey & Spice Roasted Vegetable Salad with Honey Tahini Dressing   38

Honey, Berry & Rosemary Shrub   174

Hummus & Haloumi Salad   52

Kimchi Noodles   92

Mexican Wedding Cookies   202

Okonomiyaki   104

Olive Oil, Yoghurt, Lemon & Rosemary Tea Cake   214

One Minute Mayo   168

Peanut Butter, Banana, Chocolate & Raspberry Loaf   204

Panko-Crumbed Tofu Fingers with Spicy Mayo   138

Puy Lentils & Baby Mozzarella with Basil Dressing & Roasted Cherry Tomatoes   24

Quinoa, Spring Onion & Parmesan Patties   130

Rich Mushroom & French Lentil Pie with Crunchy Filo Topping   114

Roasted Vine Tomatoes, Sourdough, Fresh Mozzarella And Green Olives   48

Seedy Yoghurt Flatbreads   166

Spelt Scones with Two Cheeses & Spinach   134

Spiced Potato Frittata with Fried Onions, Coriander & Kasundi   86

Stone Fruit And Raspberry Clafoutis   216

The Best Egg Salad   146

The Easiest One Bowl Gluten Free Pizza Base   178

Walnut, Oat & Parmesan Savoury Biscuits   136

Very Crunchy Roast Potatoes   150

Vietnamese Inspired Chicken Lettuce Cups   90

W

Walnut, Oat & Parmesan Savoury Biscuits   136

THANK YOU!

How lucky I am to find myself here, with a finished book and the chance to say thank you to the people that helped me get it into the world.

Yay for Beatnik Publishing. This has been really fun! Sally, Rachel, Kitki and Karen, I'm so grateful to you for all your hard work on this.

A big thank you to my superstar mother-in-law Susan Williams for editing my recipes with such thoughtfulness. I'm appreciative for not only that but all the culinary, garden and home inspiration you've given me over the years.

I extensively used ceramics in the book by Lily Weeds from Lil Ceramics and Lucy Leong from Salad Days. Thank you so much for making gorgeous things that make my food look great. Please go and check out their work.

Some of my wonderful clients let me include recipes and images that I created for them in the book. I appreciate this so much and am thankful for the yummy work we've made together. Thank you: All Good Bananas, Bird and Barrow, Borges Olive Oil, Cook and Nelson, The CareFillery, Nautilus Estate, NZ Avocado and Taylor Pass Honey. I have the best clients in the world.

Thank you Matt Britton, Ellie Smith and Cleo Britton for jumping in and allowing your good-looking selves to be part of a mad photoshoot day.

Sonya Nagels, you rescued me with your photography skills when I'd left some key stuff a wee bit close to deadline. Thank you so much.

Luke Williams, I did it! And thankfully, I wasn't nearly as nutty as last time was I? You've been patient and generous with your time while I worked on the book, jumping behind, and in front of the camera when I needed help. Also, thank you for your editing help with my writing when it got over-enthusiastic and unwieldy. Your opinion has been invaluable. I love you and am so grateful for you, our little family and all our meals and adventures together.

Diana and Bonnie, I can't say or write anything about you two darling girls without getting weepy. I just adore being your mum. Thank you for your enthusiasm, suggestions and feedback, your wonderful photography skills, Bonnie, and always being willing to be in photos, Diana. The cheerleading you both did was just the fuel I needed. Love you always.

First published in 2023 by Beatnik Publishing.

Text: © 2023 Kelly Gibney
Editors: Susan Williams & Rachel White

Photography: © 2023 Kelly Gibney,
with the exception of pages 8, 14 and 95 © 2023 Sonya Nagels,
pages 159 © 2023 Bonnie Williams, and 189 © 2023 Luke Williams

Design, Typesetting & Cover: © 2023 Beatnik Publishing
Publisher & Creative Direction: Sally Greer
Designer: Kitki Tong

Illustrations: Sally Greer

Font Designers: Malou Verlomme, Monotype
& Kris Sowersby, Klim Type Foundry

This book is copyright. Apart from any fair dealing for the purposes of private study, research or review, as permitted under the Copyright Act, no part may be reproduced by any process without the permission of the publishers.

Printed and bound in China using plant-based inks on Forest Stewardship Council® (FSC®)-certified paper and other controlled material in a BSCI and SEDEX certified workplace.

ISBN 978-1-99-116573-2

www.beatnikpublishing.com

PO Box 8276, Newmarket,
Auckland 1149, New Zealand